**UNDERSTANDING THE ECONOMY:
FOR PEOPLE WHO CAN'T STAND
ECONOMICS**

# UNDERSTANDING THE ECONOMY: FOR PEOPLE WHO CAN'T STAND ECONOMICS

Alfred L. Malabre, Jr.

DODD, MEAD & COMPANY   NEW YORK

Library of Congress Cataloging in Publication Data

Malabre, Alfred L
    Understanding the economy: For people who can't stand economics

    Includes index.
    1. United States—Economic conditions—
1961–      2. Economics.  I. Title.
HC106.6.M338      330.9'73'092      76-2465
ISBN 0-396-07309-3

For Mary Patricia

# ACKNOWLEDGMENTS

Many people, too many to recount, have made this book possible. My particular thanks should be expressed here, however, to Charlie Flood, an old friend and a fine writer, for his sorely needed advice early on; to Allen Klots, my editor, for his most valuable encouragement and guidance; to John O'Riley and Lindley Clark, my esteemed editorial colleagues at *The Wall Street Journal*, whose perception and wisdom have enhanced my own efforts to appreciate unfolding economic developments; and to my family for their unfailing tolerance of my often exasperating working habits during the preparation of this book.

# CONTENTS

# UNDERSTANDING THE ECONOMY: FOR PEOPLE WHO CAN'T STAND ECONOMICS

Chapter 1

# AN EXPLANATION

This book is for the person who wishes to keep reasonably well informed about economic developments. It is for the interested layman who wants to gain a little perspective on the economic headlines that come at us daily from television, radio, and the newspapers. It is for the concerned *non*expert who seeks not expertise but enough familiarity with economic data to allow an intelligent personal appraisal of where the economy stands and where it may move in future weeks and months.

This is *not* a book for anyone wishing to study the social science of economics. It is *not* a book espousing any particular economic theory. It is *not* a book for anyone who is content merely to accept what others, in high or low position, may be saying about the economy.

Most decidedly, this is *not* a textbook. Most decidedly, it urges no political point of view. The only converts it seeks are converts to a more enlightened assimilation of daily economic headlines.

Within these pages, you will find not a single formula or chart or graph. Nor will you encounter at the end any glossary of economic definitions. When you come to a term that requires defining, it will be defined on the spot.

At the end you will find an index. If you want to discover quickly what the gross national product is really all

1

about, you can look it up in the index and then flip to the appropriate pages. You will obtain, I submit, a more useful description of what the GNP actually represents than could be provided by the standard glossary-type definition that appears in textbooks.

Just as this is by no stretch of the imagination an economics textbook, I am by no stretch of the imagination a professional economist. I am a newspaperman, employed by *The Wall Street Journal*. I happen to find considerable fascination in observing and writing about the American economy. But I would be hard pressed to explain to you the difference between a regression series and a diffusion index. And I question whether you would care to have me explain. It would be a boring business.

There is nothing boring, however, about trying to understand some basic things about the nation's economy— what goes into it, what comes out of it, how we measure it, how it moves and changes, how it is influenced by the behavior of businessmen and the decisions, for better or for worse, of government officials and political leaders.

\*     \*     \*

A fundamental premise of this book is that many Americans share an interest in such matters. But another premise is that an unfortunate combination of circumstances works to discourage people from becoming better informed about the economy. Almost without exception, the few good economic textbooks available are fat and forbidding, and they generally fail to provide such elementary information as where to find and how to read basic understandable gauges of the state of the country's economy.

The unhappy result is a dearth of fundamental material for the individual—student or interested layman— who merely wants to be able to regard the economic scene with a little common sense and sophistication.

"Economics as a science is not 'dismal'—as Thomas Carlyle once called it," says Charls E. Walker, a professional economist who served as a high official in the Treasury Department from 1969 to 1973. "The problem is that it has been dismally taught—if taught at all."

Speaking of the need for a greater understanding of the economy by the electorate, Mr. Walker remarks: "It is not a job that will be over soon, but we must get on with it or wake up some day to find ourselves with an economic system that nobody wants—one that performs poorly and fails to deliver in a manner that the people of the U.S. have come to expect. If our economic system does fail, the underpinnings of our participatory democracy will indeed be weakened and the chances of fulfilling the American dream will be greatly reduced."

Tilford Gaines, senior vice-president and economist of Manufacturers Hanover Trust Co., a large New York bank, recently wrote: "It is amazing how ignorant most Americans are about the free-enterprise economic system and, particularly at the present moment, how little faith there is in its continued functioning. All educated people understand our political system and the checks and balances that have enabled it to work. All religious people understand the tenets of their faith. Each artisan or professional understands the rules of his trade. But how many understand the logical structures of our economy and importance of our economic institutions within our total social fabric?"

A recent survey shows that only about half of the nation's 60,000 social-studies teachers—those most likely to be teaching economics courses in schools—have had any formal training in economics. Another finding of the survey is that only about a quarter of the nation's junior-high-school students understand the difference between a free-enterprise economy and one that is completely government controlled.

What percentage of those students would be able to identify the Federal Open Market Committee and the fundamental role that committee plays in shaping America's economic future? My guess would be, at the most, a minuscule fraction of the 25 per cent who managed to identify free enterprise.

*    *    *

As Charls Walker suggests, the way in which basic economics is generally taught may be to blame for much of the aversion to economic matters. Too frequently, introductory courses that should simply equip students with basic tools for understanding economic developments focus instead on boring, impractical theoretical matters. That may be fine for anyone moving on with economics as the major course of study. But it is of no discernible use to the student who merely wants to be able to digest the abundant economic news and perhaps make a few intelligent judgments.

A case in point is my own classroom experience with economics at Yale University shortly after World War II. Unfortunately, the classroom scene has not changed appreciably since then. The course at Yale, Econ 10, was a half-year affair, designed for students majoring in other fields. Mine happened to be English. The course, supposedly a simple introduction to economics for students majoring in something else, consisted mainly of discussing assorted formulas and curves, drawn majestically on the classroom blackboard by the instructor. It was uninteresting in all respects; it had, so far as I could determine, not the faintest connection with the real world beyond the New Haven campus.

Benumbed and benighted, I managed—barely—to pass the course. But it remains to this day the one and only economics course that I have ever suffered through.

* * *

The economy can probably never be made as interesting as a good Alfred Hitchcock thriller. However, there is no need for it to be made dismally dull. The economy can be an intensely interesting subject—to nonexperts as well as professional economists. Moreover, it can be followed, by those willing to try, without any real difficulty. To follow it requires no long-standing scholarly comprehension of the intricate workings of the economy. But you do need common sense and a passing familiarity with what has happened in the past. No more expertise is needed than in understanding the more rudimentary baseball statistics (nothing so complicated as slugging percentages) and knowing the difference between two per cent and two percentage points.

Parenthetically: you may discover, as a dividend to a better understanding of the economy, that you will be able to invest your money more wisely. Certainly, my own economy-watching over the years has enabled me to venture out occasionally with my crystal ball. I do recall, for example, a column of mine that appeared Dec. 8, 1969—a gloomy time on Wall Street. The widely watched Dow Jones industrial-stock average stood at 785.04, down sharply from about 970 in mid-May of 1969. The economy clearly seemed headed into a recession. Unemployment was moving steadily upward. Corporate profits were sliding in the opposite direction. It hardly seemed an appropriate moment for a cheery, lighthearted appraisal of stock-market prospects. Yet, that was precisely what I produced for the *Journal*'s readers that Monday morning.

"What the stock market needs," I cheerily started out, "is a good recession; there's nothing like a business slump to perk up stock prices." The column went on to suggest, on the basis of various statistics, that a recession indeed appeared imminent and that, consequently, most stock prices appeared quite reasonable. The column went so far as to forecast that stock prices, though due for a "sustained . . . rebound" from the December, 1969, level, would probably flounder around for several months before beginning a big climb.

The record book shows that a recession did begin about that time—the National Bureau of Economic Research, official arbiter in such matters, places the start in November, 1969. The record further shows that stock prices, measured by the Dow Jones average, did flounder around until May of 1970 and then began a sustained rise, gradual at first, that brought the average to 840 by the end of 1970 and to more than 950 early the next year. Thus, my 1969 column, had its advice been taken, would have enabled an investor to pick up some 165 points on the Dow Jones index in less than 18 months.

No training in economics or finance was responsible for the accuracy of that forecast. Rather, a little common-sense research into business history was all that was necessary—research that anyone with an ability to read the English language and a mild tolerance for a few uncomplicated statistics could have undertaken. Even a cursory glance at the appropriate figures shows that stock prices often are higher at the pit of a business recession than around the peak of a preceding expansion period. In many instances, the rise in stock prices during a recession has been dramatic.

Nicholas Von Hoffman, an exceedingly able and articulate syndicated newspaper columnist, recently observed that "time was when nobody but economists and upper-echelon people in big business paid attention to economic statistics," but now "the media throw more and more of those numbers at us."

This book will enable you to understand a lot more about what is coming at you the next time an announcer or a politician or a newspaper reporter starts spouting economic statistics. A particular figure on a particular day may be important, or it may not be. In any event—most importantly—you will be able to make that judgment for yourself.

# Chapter 2

# THE HEADLINE GRABBERS

JUST WHAT do we mean when we talk about "the economy"?

We often say that the economy "looks good" or the economy "looks bad." What do we mean? What is the economy, really, and how can we keep a tab on it?

There are countless ways of looking at the economy. It encompasses an infinitely diverse range of business activity that transpires daily in the nation. A man drives from his home to his office in the morning. Along the way, he stops to buy a newspaper. At the office, he goes to the cafeteria and purchases a cup of coffee. Back at his desk, he picks up the phone and places a long-distance call to an associate in a city 2,000 miles away.

As far as the man is concerned, only the phone call is directly a part of his business endeavors. But in the larger picture—as far as the overall U.S. economy is concerned—every one of his actions contributes to the nation's general level of economic activity. The drive to the office, buying the newspaper, the coffee, and the telephone call all tend to expand overall economic activity. All are a part—albeit a minuscule fraction—of what we really are talking about when we mention "the economy."

To go from such tiny segments of the nation's economic scene to surveying the entire economy with reason-

able intelligence requires a familiarity with some basic statistics compiled largely by highly trained analysts in
various branches of the Federal government, particularly
in the Commerce Department, the Labor Department,
the Federal Reserve Board, and the Treasury Department. Each of these government divisions issues wide-
ranging data that help give us, if we merely know where
to look and how to look, a better grasp of the overall economic picture.

## People

There is an old saw that defines the difference between
a recession and a depression thus: *A recession is when your
neighbor is unemployed and a depression is when you are unemployed.*

A better way to see whether the economy is in a recession or depression, or neither, is to take a look at the nation's overall unemployment rate. This is issued on a
monthly basis by the Labor Department's Bureau of
Labor Statistics in Washington. The BLS also provides
monthly reports on the level of unemployment within
various categories of the labor force—adult men, adult
women, teenagers, married men, blacks and other minority races, whites, white-collar workers, blue-collar workers, nonagricultural workers, construction workers,
workers who manufacture such "durable" goods as
automobiles and appliances, and so on and so on.

A glance at the BLS report will show whether 4 per
cent, 6 per cent, 8 per cent, 10 per cent or whatever portion of the labor force is unemployed during a given
month—that is, wants work but can't find work. The BLS
report even carries the unemployment rate out to one
decimal point for all the categories. The report also

shows the trend of joblessness: Whether the latest month's rate is higher or lower, for example, than a month earlier or a year earlier. It also provides absolute figures for the various worker categories, along with the percentages.

It's possible, in a given month, for instance, to have the unemployment rate rise at the same time that the number of jobholders in the country rises. The explanation can simply be that the number of persons entering the labor force and seeking work rose more sharply than usual in the particular month. This is precisely what happened, for example, between August and September of 1974. In that period, the overall unemployment rate jumped from 5.4 per cent of the labor force to 5.8 per cent. At first glance, the rise in joblessness suggests a deterioration in the country's labor situation. However, a closer inspection of BLS figures turns up the fact—not mentioned in the black headlines of rising unemployment—that employment also climbed substantially during the period, from 86,187,000 to 86,538,000—a rise in jobholders of about 350,000 in a single month. A further perusal of BLS statistics for the period provides a clear explanation of the paradox. The percentage of the country's working-age population employed or seeking work climbed from 61.7 per cent in August to 62.1 per cent in September. That percentage rise may seem insignificantly small, but it translates into a rise in the country's total labor force of nearly 800,000 persons. A major factor, of course, is the rising number of American women who wish to work.

In sum, a close look at all the job statistics, not just the overall unemployment rate, shows that the economy actually provided substantially more jobs during the period. However, the increase was not swift enough to accommodate the sharp rise in persons seeking work.

The lesson, clearly, for anyone wishing to gain a reasonable perspective on this important facet of economic activity, is that it pays to inspect more than simply the raw BLS figure for the overall unemployment rate.

Yet, unhappily, it is this raw figure that always seems to grab the headlines, even in newspapers that should know better and that try to provide their readers with a balanced picture of the country's actual labor situation. In the end, all too often, it is the raw figure that stirs passions in Congress and on Main Street, and ultimately provokes legislative and other action in Washington that again and again in the recent past has led to overstimulation of business in well-intentioned but questionable efforts to reduce unemployment.

An illustration of this tendency occurred early in 1975. In figures released by the BLS in early February, the overall unemployment rate took a particularly sharp jump, to 8.2 per cent of the labor force in January from 7.2 per cent in December. The headlines were even bigger and blacker than usual. The Ford administration, which until then had seemed reluctant to adopt economic policies that might possibly risk a revival of severe inflation in the country, came under sharp attack from all sorts of opinion leaders. George Meany, the president of the powerful A.F.L.–C.I.O., expressed outrage that President Ford was not taking drastic action to curb the climbing joblessness.

Within less than a week, as the criticism from Mr. Meany and others continued to mount, President Ford began to alter his previous cautious economic stance. On Feb. 11, for example, only four days after the BLS report of 8.2 per cent unemployment, the President dramatically announced that he would release some $2 billion of impounded highway construction funds to help create jobs.

The President's abrupt decision shows how a single economic statistic can command the headlines and, if it generates enough public clamor, can directly alter the course of Washington policy, and ultimately the course of the economy and, possibly, the nation. The wisdom of Mr. Ford's decision, of course, could be challenged on the ground that it encouraged highway building at a time when the nation was attempting, not very successfully, to conserve fuel. But it could also be challenged for another reason, one that could only be perceived by persons willing to read well beyond the black headlines of 8.2 per cent unemployment. The details of the January job figures showed that the unemployment rate for heads of households, the family breadwinners, rose only to 5.2 per cent from 4.6 per cent in December. The rate for married men rose only to 4.5 per cent from 3.8 per cent. And the so-called hardship unemployment rate, people out of work 15 weeks or more, inched up to 1.7 per cent from 1.4 per cent. Unemployment among persons out of work 27 weeks or more held at less than 1 per cent—to be exact, 0.7 per cent—hardly the sort of level that Mr. Meany's outraged cries would lead one to anticipate.

Remarking on such little-noticed statistics, Albert H. Cox Jr., chief economist of Lionel D. Edie & Co., a New York investment research concern owned by Merrill Lynch, Pierce, Fenner & Smith, Inc., the world's largest stock-brokerage house, wrote at the time: "News media and politicians are continuing to exaggerate and distort the issue of unemployment. With the release of last month's estimated total unemployment rate of 8.2 per cent, headlines created visions of the Great Depression and all its extreme hardships. The facts . . . clearly contradict such impressions, but the illusion is leading both the Administration and Congress to over-react by spending too much money, a significant portion of which will not be covered by taxation. . . . This raises the threat of another boom–bust cycle."

On the same day that Mr. Cox made his comments, a short news item appeared in *The Wall Street Journal.* It carried no large headlines and received scant attention. It reported that "low-status jobs remain hard to fill, despite surging unemployment." One "key reason for the situation," the *Journal* article stated, appeared to be that many of the jobless were able to get along adequately on unemployment insurance, food stamps and welfare. The article went on to report, for example, that a Chicago taxi company found that applications for hard-to-fill cabbie jobs declined whenever "President Ford announced new unemployment benefits." Also noting this phenomenon, Lionel Edie's Mr. Cox declared that "unemployment and welfare benefits have now risen to the point where they create unemployment."

\*    \*    \*

At this point, it may be worth inserting a few parenthetical words about just how the BLS obtains its unemployment statistics. Briefly, pollsters hired by the Census Bureau, a branch of the Commerce Department, each month canvass about 47,000 households scattered across the nation.

Julius Shiskin, as commissioner of the BLS, has explained how this process works. The pollsters, mostly women working part time, go to these households and ask various questions. After the initial interview, followup interviews are conducted by telephone, with follow-up questions that help determine such matters as degree of hardship, duration of unemployment and so on.

"If I were given a large amount of extra money, I

would get more details on unemployment in local areas,"
Mr. Shiskin told a recent interviewer from *U.S. News &
World Report*. "Today, the unemployment figures are
being used for allocating billions of dollars' worth of
manpower revenue funds—federal money going out to
localities to be used for manpower training and public-
service jobs. Still, we are having to estimate local-area
unemployment all over the country on the basis of a
47,000-household national sample. We recently got
money to add some 13,000 households to our monthly
survey, and that will eventually give us better data."

A sample question from the pollsters: "Is anyone here
looking for a job?" According to Mr. Shiskin, the BLS
counts as unemployed anyone who is not employed and
has actively looked for a job in the preceding four weeks
but hasn't managed to land one.

This procedure leads to including among the jobless
such persons as, for example, a housewife who may be
looking for a job between 1 P.M. and 4 P.M. on week-
days, or a college student seeking work for two weeks
during his Christmas vacation.

At the other end of the spectrum, I should add, are
the so-called discouraged unemployed, who have given
up job-hunting and, when surveyed by the Census
Bureau people, may answer that no, they haven't been
job-seeking during the last four weeks. These unfortunate individuals, numbering more than a million in 1975,
according to rough BLS estimates, are not included in the
official, overall unemployment figures. The category unquestionably does include thousands of helpless cases.
However, BLS analysts estimate, it also includes countless
individuals who have become "discouraged" from job-
hunting simply because, for example, they can't find
work that they deem commensurate with their inflated

ideas of their own abilities. It is lamentable that no governmental agency compiles and issues any statistical index that shows the number of job vacancies in the country. Preliminary work toward such an index was undertaken in the early 1970s. But the project was abandoned. Some observers say it was dropped more for political reasons— to assuage minority groups and Congressional liberals— than for any technical difficulties in compiling such a yardstick.

The survey technique of the BLS has obvious advantages. It seeks to ensure that our unemployment statistics don't overlook most persons who really are jobless. But another result, many analysts believe, is that on balance it tends to inflate U.S. unemployment levels, particularly when they are compared, as they often are, to those in other major industrial countries.

In Britain, for example, unemployment rates are based on the actual number of persons who take the trouble to go to government facilities and register themselves as being out of work and wanting a job. It has been estimated that British unemployment rates, if they were calculated using the U.S. method, would be approximately twice as high as they actually are in the official British reports. This is something to bear in mind, quite obviously, when you read that U.S. unemployment stands at, say, 8 per cent of the labor force, while the jobless rate in the United Kingdom, with all its recent economic troubles, comes only to, say, 4 per cent.

To place our unemployment statistics in proper international perspective, it is also important to consider particular categories of unemployment. Joblessness among American teenagers during much of 1975 exceeded 20 per cent. Unemployment among teenagers in Britain, as well as many other lands, simply isn't regularly broken out of the overall unemployment figures. Occasional studies, however, indicate that teenage unemployment abroad runs sharply below U.S. levels. In Britain, for example, only 8,591 teenagers were registered as unemployed in mid-1974; other estimates showed that close to 2.2 million teenagers held down British jobs. Such figures indicate that teenage joblessness in Britain runs under the 1 per cent level.

In the U.S., even unemployment among black teenagers is carefully calculated each month. The jobless rate for this age–race category in recent years has crossed above the horrendous 40 per cent level. America's high teenage-unemployment rates for whites and blacks indicate that the country's sampling method of arriving at jobless statistics isn't the only reason that the U.S. labor picture seems relatively dismal. Another reason, it would seem, is that an important segment of the U.S. labor force—the teenagers, and especially the black teenagers—appears to suffer extraordinarily high joblessness. The relatively high U.S. level seems particularly distressing when one also considers that a far higher percentage of teenagers finish high school and go on to college in America than in Britain or most countries. Fewer than 3 per cent of the British population hold university degrees. Roughly 10 per cent of the U.S. population hold such degrees.

Regarding the problem of high teenage joblessness in the U.S., another noteworthy consideration in any international comparison is that the U.S. has on the books a minimum wage statute that applies to teenagers as well as older workers. Recently, some U.S. officials tried to extract from Congress a change in minimum-wage regulations that would have allowed slightly lower minimums for teenage workers than for adults. The proposal was bitterly opposed by organized labor in the U.S., particularly by the powerful A.F.L.–C.I.O. and its Mr. Meany. Apparently the labor chieftains feared that their breadwinner members, their prime constituents, might ultimately lose some jobs to lesser paid teenage competition.

It cannot be proved beyond a doubt that the inclusion of teenagers among those fully covered by minimumwage regulations is the major reason that teenage joblessness runs so high in the U.S. But there certainly may be a good deal more than a slight connection. Anyone who has had to engage a teenager for an odd summer job knows the problems involved. All too often, you end up mowing the lawn yourself or letting the sand traps on the local golf course go unraked.

At the start of 1976, the minimum wage for most workers in the U.S. rose to $2.30 an hour, the latest in a long line of increases in the wage floor dating back to 1938, when the concept of a minimum wage—25 cents an hour, as it happened—was originally put into law. The latest boost represents a 20-cent-per-hour increase, almost as much in absolute terms as the original 1938 minimum. Workers not yet up to the $2.30 minimum—but scheduled to be there no later than the start of 1978, according to law already on the books—include such job categories as farm workers and domestic help, a group that has remained in short supply (like those Chicago cab drivers) even in recent times of high overall unemployment levels. In no instance, however, is the minimum even now less than $2 an hour. Teenagers are covered by a minimum, according to the type of work they perform.

Would teenage unemployment—and therefore overall unemployment—be less if minimum wage levels did not extend to teenagers, or were lower for teenagers? Economic history certainly suggests so. In 1953, for example, when teenage unemployment averaged only 7.6 per cent, or just over double the overall jobless rate, the minimum wage was only 75 cents an hour, and various job categories in which teenagers could readily work—for instance, on the farm and in the home—were excluded from minimum wage regulations.

How many American teenagers today spend their summers in idleness, possibly developing bad habits and getting into trouble with their families and even the law, simply because there is little or no gainful employment available for them at the minimum wage? The sand traps go unraked.

The contrast to circumstances in most foreign countries is striking. In Britain, as well as many other places, there is no general minimum wage. Those minimums that do exist are agreements ironed out between powerful unions and particular employers. One, deemed among the toughest in Britain, requires that men laborers receive no less than 70 cents an hour. As far as teenagers are concerned, the only restrictions are that the youngster who works must be at least 13 years old and cannot perform work during school hours or work that is so arduous that injuries could result. "A teenager could work in a shop in London for tuppence if he were willing," comments Ann Allison of the British Information Service in New York.

The situation abroad is another thing, obviously, to keep in mind when you next ponder a gloomy headline about high teenage unemployment in the U.S.

Altogether, we can see from this look behind and around the U.S. unemployment headlines that the state of the economy—recession, depression or neither—involves far more than simply who happens to be unemployed, you, your child, your neighbor, or the fellow down the street. The big picture can indeed be glimpsed—but this must be done with much caution and in the fullest possible perspective. The necessary statistics, most of them turned out monthly by the BLS, are there for those willing to take a little time to look.

As a very rough rule of thumb, some economists draw the line between a recession and a depression by whether the overall unemployment rate is less than a double-digit figure. If unemployment comes to 9 per cent of the labor force, some analysts would say, the economy is only in a recession. But if it reaches or exceeds the 10 per cent mark, they would place the economy in a state of depression. To put the matter in perspective: Unemployment reached about 25 per cent of the labor force during the pit of the Great Depression of the 1930s, and the rate remained in double digits until World War II was under way for the U.S. Using double-digit unemployment as a yardstick of economic health, the Great Depression ran throughout the entire decade of the 1930s, encompassing, as we shall see in a later chapter, two extensive periods of business "recovery" as well as two periods of severely contracting economic activity.

## Products

The labor situation is often the first thing that pops into mind, and into the headlines, when questions arise about the health of the economy. This is doubly true if unemployment happens to strike close to home. But there are other ways of keeping a tab on the big economic picture. Another headline grabber—one that many economists scrutinize far more thoroughly than the unemployment figures—is the gross national product, or the GNP, a supposedly all-encompassing economic figure turned out by Washington's statistical mills. A simple and somewhat superficial definition of the GNP can be readily devised. It is nothing less than the estimated value in the marketplace of the country's total output of goods and services. To quote from a study by the Federal Reserve Bank of Philadelphia, entitled *The Mystery of Economic Growth,* when the GNP "goes up, most people think we are growing—the economy is producing more, they say." Paul A. Samuelson—the widely read professor of economics at Massachusetts Institute of Technology, Nobel prize-winner, and *Newsweek* columnist on business matters—has called the GNP "one of the most important concepts in all economics" because it "measures the economic performance of the whole economy."

The GNP is "gross," all right. In 1975, it approximated $1.5 trillion. A trillion, in case you have forgotten or aren't familiar with such lofty numbers, is one with a dozen zeroes after it.

Unlike the unemployment rate, the GNP figure comes out only once a quarter and invariably has to be revised and revised and revised, sometimes over many years, as Washington statisticians strive to make their estimates of past economic activity levels more precise and accurate. GNP data is compiled and issued by the Commerce Department. Like the BLS, the Commerce Department is a primary government source for the broad-gauge sort of data that help us to grasp the overall condition of the economy. A close look at the Commerce Department figures makes it easy to understand why the GNP is generally regarded as the ultimate single measure of the total economic situation. Its components—the categories that made up the $1.5 trillion figure in 1975—include all major areas of business endeavor.

The vast scope of the GNP coverage can be indicated by reviewing in very general terms the major categories that Commerce Department analysts add together to arrive at an overall figure. The first and largest, accounting for nearly two-thirds of GNP, is a category embracing all consumer spending in the country. It, in turn, is divided into three subgroups, "durable" goods such as automobiles, appliances, and furniture, "nondurable" goods such as clothing, food, and fuel, and "services" such as home-maintenance and transportation expenses.

The second major GNP category covers nongovernmental investment-type spending for everything from machine tools to new factories to warehouse supplies. This category accounts for just over 10 per cent of the GNP.

The third major GNP category takes into account all government outlays. This category, which is divided into federal defense spending, other federal spending, and expenditures by state and local governments, amounts to roughly one quarter of the GNP.

The fourth category that makes up the GNP figure embraces U.S. exports and imports of goods and services. If the export total happens to exceed the import total at a particular time, the difference is added to the GNP figure; if not, the difference is subtracted.

Generally, this difference—called the country's balance of trade—is tiny in terms of the other major GNP categories. As we will discover later, however, the balance of trade carries a significance that far exceeds its apparently minor importance in the GNP statistics.

\*　　\*　　\*

If we may return momentarily to our friend going to work, we can see where his various activities fit into the makeup of the GNP. His purchase of the car that he drives to work shows up in the durable goods subgroup of the consumer spending category. The gasoline consumed on the way to work is in the same major category, but under the nondurable subgroup. So are the newspapers and the cup of coffee. The cost of the long-distance telephone call comes under the services subgroup. The cost of buying business equipment in his office falls into the large category that includes nongovernmental spending. If our man happened to be working for, say, the Commerce Department instead of a private concern, the equipment would show up under the large GNP category covering government outlays, in the subgroup for expenditures for other than defense purposes.

Just as unemployment figures have to be viewed with caution, so do GNP statistics—but for very different reasons. Unemployment figures, of course, involve numbers of people. But GNP data, as we have already seen, are expressed in terms of American dollars. And American dollars, unlike American people, have shrunk rather drastically over the years since World War II—on account of inflation. The upshot is that GNP statistics can provide a very misleading view of the overall economy if they are not somehow adjusted to allow for inflation. For instance, 1974 is conceded to have been a year of sharply contracting business activity in the U.S. Yet, the country's GNP actually rose by nearly $100 billion during the year.

That hardly sounds like an economy in trouble. The trouble shows up when the figures are adjusted for rising prices. The adjusted GNP figure that results is, appropriately, called the "real" GNP, and it certainly seems to be a good deal more realistic than the unadjusted GNP figure, at least in inflationary times.

Let us take another look at the 1974 record using the real GNP as the yardstick. This economic yardstick actually declined on the order of $40 billion during the year—a far cry from the huge increase of $100 billion registered by the unadjusted GNP figure.

The adjustment process used by Commerce Department statisticians is a complicated matter and will not be detailed here. Briefly, however, it can be stated that the statisticians attempt to adjust for inflation throughout the economy, at all levels of transaction; not just, say, at the consumer price level, where you or I might enter the picture when we buy food at the supermarket or clothing or appliances at the store.

As a result of such efforts, the real GNP unquestionably provides a much clearer picture of the general economic health of the nation than the unadjusted figure. But even the real GNP has its drawbacks and should not be taken unquestioningly as the ultimate measure of where the economy stands.

The validity of the real GNP—as well as of the unadjusted GNP figure from which it is largely derived—hinges on the accuracy of the diverse statistics that comprise it. The GNP concept is so all-inclusive that it is also, unavoidably, vulnerable to large miscalculations and downright errors in the course of its compilation.

Oskar Morgenstern, a noted economics professor who has conducted highly critical analyses of GNP data over the years, may have overstated the case only slightly when he recently told an audience at New York University: "Alas, the GNP concept is primitive in the extreme." Many of his complaints about the statistic cannot be denied. He correctly noted, for example, that "many services are rendered and many goods are produced that never enter a market" and therefore never show up anywhere in any of the categories or subsections of the GNP.

A delightful absurdity in the GNP concept, remarked upon by Dr. Morgenstern and others, is that the household duties performed by housewives—cooking, cleaning and the like—are nowhere considered in GNP data. Yet, if the same duties are performed by a hired maid, the services subsection of consumer spending accordingly increases, giving a small feminine boost to the overall economy—at least as it is represented by the GNP measures, real or unadjusted for price changes. It is not entirely facetious to contend that the economy, as described by GNP or real GNP statistics, would tend to expand appreciably faster than it has done in recent years if every wife in the country simply hired herself out as a maid to work for the family next door.

Another problem with the GNP concept, as Dr. Morgenstern and other analysts have observed, is that it records as positive contributions to overall economic activity events that really represent a malfunctioning of the economic system. Dr. Morgenstern uses this illustration:

"If we are stuck in one of the thousands of traffic jams, if airplanes are stacked and cannot land on schedule, if fires break out and other disasters occur that require repair—up goes the GNP. More gasoline is used, fares go up, overtime has to be paid, and so on. It would be difficult in any other science [than economics] to find a measure which tells simultaneously opposite stories of the functioning of a complex system in one . . . number. If we merely improve the scheduling of airplanes and stagger the times of automobile traffic, and nothing else is changed—down goes GNP. It goes up, on the other hand, if industry pollutes the air and we create other industries which remove the polluting substances."

## Prices

A third key feature of the overall economic scene that has managed in recent years to grab headlines with impressive regularity is the subject of inflation. Indeed, in the late 1960s and early 1970s, it seems safe to say that no other facet of the economy—for good reason—attracted such attention. It also may be said, however, that keeping an accurate tab on inflation can be every bit as tricky as maintaining a clear view of the labor situation or the true position of the gross national product.

When people talk about "inflation" and when a newspaper headline proclaims PRICES CLIMB TO RECORD LEVEL, this refers normally to the latest consumer price report of the BLS, the same government statistics mill that puts out, as we have observed, the unemployment rate.

That aforementioned fellow who drives to work, buys a newspaper and coffee and makes a phone call from his office, may read on the front page of his newspaper that inflation is getting worse. If his newspaper happens to cost him more than, say, the day before, he will have dramatic, first-hand evidence of worsening inflation. In any event, if he reads much beyond that inflation headline, the chances are he will find that the fine print of the article actually reports that the BLS index of consumer prices a month ago rose above its level in the preceding month.

Unfortunately, such articles seldom go into much detail about the movement of different items comprising the consumer price index, or simply the CPI. But the BLS does in fact provide considerable detail with regard to individual items. In the monthly reports of the BLS, the CPI is broken down into three major categories—food, other commodities, and services. These categories, in turn, are broken down. The food category, for instance, shows monthly price trends for such diverse items as cereals, bakery products, meats, poultry, fish, dairy products, fruits, vegetables, and, in a special subsection, food eaten away from home. The category embracing all other commodities is split into three parts—all nondurable goods, nondurable foods other than clothing, and durable goods. Each of these parts is further divided into subsections covering such diverse items as gasoline, motor oil, tobacco products, alcoholic beverages, fuel oil and coal. The third major CPI category, covering services, provides price information on rent, medical care, and transit fares, among others.

The BLS also provides monthly price information for different urban areas. At the same time that the bureau releases its overall consumer price data for the nation as a whole each month, it reports in detail the consumer-price trend in Chicago, Detroit, the Los Angeles–Long Beach area, the New York–Northeastern New Jersey area, and Philadelphia. It also issues full, quarterly consumer price statistics for Boston, Houston, Minneapolis–St. Paul, Pittsburgh, Buffalo, Cleveland, Dallas, Milwaukee, San Diego, Seattle, Washington, Atlanta, Baltimore, Cincinnati, Honolulu, Kansas City, St. Louis, and the San Francisco–Oakland area.

The CPI is based on prices of approximately 400 items that BLS analysts have chosen to represent the movement of prices of all goods and services purchased by wage earners and clerical workers in urban areas—which by definition includes residents of towns with as few as 2,500 people. Prices for these items are collected by shoppers trained by the BLS. They buy at some 18,000 business establishments around the country, including grocery and department stores, hospitals, filling stations, and the like. Mailed questionnaires are also used by the bureau to keep track of price trends involving such items as local transit fares and public-utility rates. The CPI expresses its monthly index in terms of the average price level prevailing during 1967, the so-called base year for many economic indexes. The report that the CPI stood at 156.1 in January, 1975, for example, is another way of saying that consumer prices, on the average, rose 56.1 per cent between 1967 and January, 1975.

The relative importance assigned in the monthly index to individual items is based on a BLS study of the spending habits of some 10,000 families. A major criticism of the index is that such studies are conducted only once a decade, and occasionally not even that often. The criticism, clearly valid, holds that consumer spending habits change more frequently, and that unless these changes are monitored more often the CPI becomes increasingly misleading. BLS officials claim that a limited budget precludes more regular studies.

In any event, occasional updating does take place. Recently, BLS analysts were assigning an importance, or "weight," of about 25 per cent to food, 39 per cent to nonfood commodities, and 36 per cent to services, within the overall CPI. This is a change from, say, 1970, when food's weight, for instance, was only 22 per cent. In attempting to keep the index as realistic as possible, the BLS in recent years has also made changes in items monitored. It has begun pricing, among other things, between-meal snacks, motel rooms, garbage disposal units, moving expenses, parking fees, taxi fares, outboard motors, golf fees, college tuition, music lessons, legal fees, and funeral charges. At the same time, items dropped from the list, on the theory that they now constitute too minor a part of consumer spending patterns, include lemons, nightgowns, pajamas, appendectomies and sewing machines.

Other unpriced expenses, which some critics claim should be taken into account, include income taxes, personal property taxes and Social Security taxes. Sales and real estate taxes, however, are regularly measured by BLS samplers.

The importance of the CPI, it should be noted, extends far beyond simply providing us with a means of keeping track of inflation. Incomes of roughly half the U.S. population are linked, through so-called escalator clauses in labor contracts and other pay arrangements, to changes in the CPI. Affected are some 30 million Social Security beneficiaries, roughly 15 million food-stamp recipients, some six million workers covered by union contracts, more than two million U.S. Civil Service and military retirees, and close to one million postal workers, among others. In addition, such other matters as alimony and child-support payments often are tied to changes in the CPI.

"An increase of only 1 per cent in the index results in some $1 billion in additional wages and other payments to the American people," estimates a recent study by Towers, Perrin, Forster & Crosby, a Philadelphia-based management-consulting firm. The report adds: "Because the cost of living and inflation have become the Siamese twins of modern-day economic discussion, it is vital to understand what the CPI is, what it is not, and what it should be."

With an eye to improving its consumer price data, and mindful of the huge importance of the statistics to so many people, the BLS has recently been conducting surveys aimed at producing still more accurate information. Starting in the spring of 1977, according to current plans, the bureau will publish two consumer price indexes—the present one, which covers urban wage earners and clerical workers, and a new one, which will cover the entire urban population, or about 80 per cent of all Americans.

The new index will be called the "Consumer Price Index for All Urban Households." This would fill a major void in the current index—the fact that it doesn't take into account the spending habits of executives, professionals, the well-to-do, the very poor, and other urban dwellers who are neither wage earners nor clerical personnel. Farmers, a shrinking segment of the population, would be among the few population categories still not covered in the forthcoming index.

In passing: A delightful, semiserious attempt to gauge cost-of-living trends for the currently excluded well-to-do has already been made by Raymond F. DeVoe Jr., a senior vice-president of Spencer Trask & Co., a New York securities concern. Mr. DeVoe, a gentleman well known along Wall Street for the whimsy that he manages to inject into matters economic, has worked up something that he calls the "Cost of Living It Up Index," or simply the CLIUI. Mr. DeVoe's index, based on his own experiences in New York, as well as on reports from his wealthier cocktail-party acquaintances, covers price trends of such items as caviar, Pucci scarves, maids, private schools, mink coats, maintenance charges in large Park Avenue apartments, Brooks Brothers neckties, Countess Mara neckties, summer camps in Maine, annual tuition at Harvard, veterinarians' fees, silver baby cups at Tiffany, gold jewelry, a shoeshine with tip, employing a bartender at home, employing Jim Buck dog-walkers, a ticket to see the New York Knicks, a ticket to see a Broadway musical, dinner at Le Mistral, a Beefeater martini, *The Monthly Labor Review*, a parlor-car ticket on the Cannonball train from New York to Southampton, and annual dues at the University Club.

In all, 72 items are included in Mr. DeVoe's CLIUI, which in a recent twelve-month period soared about 20 per cent, he estimates, or roughly twice as rapidly as the far less fascinating CPI climbed in the same twelve months. If nothing else, Mr. DeVoe's research suggests that the recent BLS decision to begin taking account of the spending habits of the well-to-do could alter the behavior of the bureau's overall price data, by giving it an upward push.

The economic impact of relatively minor alterations in the CPI was pointed out vividly in a 1975 article in *Barron's,* a weekly business magazine, titled "Figures Do Lie." In December, 1974, the article recalled, the BLS discovered that it had erred slightly in its monthly CPI report, so that the reported index was one-tenth of a point higher than it should have been. That hardly sounds like a very significant miscalculation, but *Barron's* noted that if the error had been allowed to stand it would have meant, in the course of a year, an overpayment of a penny an hour to, among others, 10,000 employees of Kennecott Copper Corp. It would have cost the company, many of whose employees are covered by the aforementioned escalator clauses in their labor contracts, more than $200,000.

Altogether, it's not in the least surprising that the CPI is the most widely followed measure of inflation. It is broad-ranging and readily comprehensible. But it is a fact that not all economists turn first to the CPI when they wish to ascertain the economy's overall price situation—broad as it is, the CPI is not the most comprehensive price yardstick available. That distinction belongs to a far less renowned inflation gauge, one that rarely makes the headlines. It is called, somewhat forbiddingly, the GNP price deflator.

\* \* \*

Unlike the monthly CPI, the GNP deflator is issued only quarterly, and not by the BLS but by the Commerce

Department. And despite its forbidding name, it is not really that complicated a statistic. Essentially, it is a measure of the difference between the GNP and the real GNP. It is obtained simply by dividing the GNP for a given period by the real GNP for the same period. When this division has been performed, it is possible to see whether the GNP deflator has been rising or falling and at what rate. It's worth noting that the movement of the deflator usually closely parallels the movement of the CPI but is rarely identical to it. In 1974, for example, the CPI rose about 11 per cent and the deflator about 10 per cent. One explanation for the difference is that the year's inflationary pressures were more heavily concentrated in prices at retail than at other levels of business, such as at the factory and in the warehouse. Because it takes all these levels into account, the deflator tended to rise slightly less than the CPI, whose complete focus is on retail transactions.

The GNP deflator is the most comprehensive inflation yardstick almost by definition—precisely because it is derived from the GNP itself, which, as we have noted, constitutes the broadest statistical measure we have of overall economic activity. Thus, the GNP deflator, at least in theory, reflects price trends throughout the country's economy, not just at the neighborhood store. Of course, we have also seen that the GNP concept has its limits, and those shortcomings necessarily limit the accuracy of the deflator as a price yardstick.

\*    \*    \*

Although the CPI and the GNP deflator are the two main means by which experts—and nonexperts—can keep reasonably up to date on general price developments within the economy, there are several other useful indexes that deserve attention. The first of these is the so-called wholesale price index, which, like the CPI, is published monthly by the BLS. The wholesale price index, or WPI, gives an extensive breakdown of specific items, as the CPI does. The list includes such categories as farm products, industrial commodities, and such "special" groups as items processed for eventual sale to consumers. The monthly WPI reports contain enormous detail about individual products. For example, under a subcategory called "non-metallic mineral products" we find this further breakdown: Flat glass, concrete ingredients, concrete products, structural clay products, refractory products, asphalt roofing, gypsum products, and glass containers and other nonmetallic minerals.

BLS statisticians break the WPI down in other ways as well. One is by stage of processing. The subgroups here include crude materials in need of further processing, intermediate materials, and finished goods. The finished-goods section is further broken down into consumer-finished goods, such as washing machines, and producer-finished goods, such as machine tools.

For all its store of price information, however, the WPI does not—in fact, by definition, cannot—provide a measurement of price trends in the service sector of the economy, an increasingly important area covered by both the CPI and the GNP deflator. Measurement of the service sector is essential to any complete view of the country's price picture. Another problem with the WPI—with which BLS officials have recently been wrestling—is the fact that, unlike the CPI's, its monthly prices are often based on the quoted, official selling prices of manufacturers, or on prices quoted on organized exchanges or markets. The index fails to measure excise taxes and, more importantly, it frequently fails to take into account discounts from quoted prices that are common in wholesale transactions, particularly at times when business demand may be weak.

Other areas not measured in the WPI include construction, real estate, transportation, securities, printing, publishing and goods produced for the military establishment. In fact, sales by the federal government generally are excluded from the WPI.

Despite its shortcomings, however, the WPI does offer one important advantage over the CPI of the GNP deflator. It often tends to foreshadow trends that subsequently develop in the other two price indexes. The WPI, for instance, began dropping in late 1974 and continued to fall in early 1975, presaging an easing of the upward spiral in both the CPI and the deflator. In a very rough sense, then, the WPI can be viewed as a "leading indicator"—the term used by economic forecasters—of broader trends to come in the overall economy. There are many very much better leading indicators of general economic activity, and they will presently be reviewed in detail.

There are also quite a few other yardsticks of price trends, besides the three major ones described above. The most important, perhaps, is a little-known BLS index showing the average price level of a small, specially selected group of industrial raw materials. This weekly index, called simply the index of industrial materials prices, has proved to be a far better precursor of price trends than even the WPI. It will be discussed in a later chapter, along with other important leading indicators.

Suffice it now to say that BLS economists chose the 13 raw materials that comprise the index with a special eye to finding items whose prices tend to react sharply and promptly to incipient but far-reaching forces under way in the economy. In late 1974 and early 1975, for example, when the WPI was cautiously edging lower and the CPI and the deflator were merely beginning to rise more slowly, the raw-materials price index was declining sharply—and had been for many months. Anyone familiar with the index, which is readily available through BLS reports, would have gained a useful and uncommon insight into inflation prospects and the outlook for the economy.

Chapter 3

# SUBTLER SIGNS

WE HAVE seen in the previous chapter the importance of looking behind the familiar headlines that proclaim changes in such eye-catching, broad-gauge statistics
as the unemployment rate, the gross national product
and the consumer price index. Understanding something
about the nature of these headline grabbers—what goes
into them, their strengths and their weaknesses—constitutes a big step toward an appreciation of what the economy, that often-used but seldom-defined term, is really
all about.

A familiarity with some other yardsticks—ones that
make the front pages less frequently—helps provide additional perspective on the shape and nature of the economy.

## Living Standards

Knowing about the job situation or where the GNP
stands or how fast the CPI happens to be climbing at a
particular time doesn't tell us all that we may want to
know about just how living standards across the country
are faring. Is the standard of living of most Americans
getting better or worse? In a sense, we are interested in
the state of the overall economy precisely because we

want to know what's really happening to our living standards. Unfortunately, however, there is no monthly figure produced by any of Washington's mills, or by anything else, that will tell us exactly where, on a nationwide basis, our standard of living actually stands, or just how it may have changed from the preceding month or quarter or year.

Our friend driving to work may feel that his standard of living is rising or falling, depending on a variety of details possibly known only to him. His car may be bigger and more powerful than the one that he drove a year ago. Possibly he has moved to a larger house. Perhaps his salary has increased. He can afford to take his wife to dinner and the movies three times a week; a year ago such outings had to be limited to once a week. They eat steak more and chicken less. Their two children now attend private schools; a year ago they were at public schools. This year's vacation will be at Montego Bay; last year's was at Atlantic City. And this year's will be a week longer.

There no doubt are some readers who question whether our friend's standard of living has really risen at all. Who needs a bigger car, anyway? It soaks up more gasoline and is generally more troublesome to keep. Who needs steak? Our man's cholesterol count already is on the high side. Chicken might be better for his health. As for schools, it can be argued that public ones in the long run offer youngsters the best preparation for getting along in times as egalitarian as these.

It is clear that a considerable amount of subjectivity is involved when we start talking about living standards. And, as we shall see, that holds whether one considers the living standard of a particular individual, such as our friend going to Montego Bay, or of the country in general. And yet it is possible to construct a rough definition of living standards with the use of some little-publicized but readily available economic yardsticks.

One statistical series that provides such information, and the one that probably receives the most attention, is a monthly report by the BLS bearing the ungainly title: "Spendable Average Weekly Earnings per Production Worker on Payrolls of Private Nonagricultural Establishments, expressed in constant dollars." Like the CPI, this series is broken down in various ways. It provides data by field of work—mining, construction, manufacturing, transportation, public utilities, wholesale and retail trade, finance, insurance, real estate, and other services. It also gives data by major regions of the country.

The index amounts to a measure of the purchasing power of weekly paychecks. To get at this, BLS economists first adjust gross weekly pay figures for price changes. For instance, if average weekly pay rises 10 per cent, but prices also rise an average of 10 per cent, the price-adjusted paycheck level remains unchanged—and hence the term "constant" dollars. But the BLS does not stop there. To get closer to true paycheck buying power, the bureau further adjusts the weekly average to take taxes into account. Accordingly, estimated federal income and Social Security taxes also are deducted from the gross figure.

As a result of such tinkering, we are able to obtain a much more realistic picture of the real worth of our paychecks—the amount of goods and services that they can buy—than would otherwise be the case. For example, in a recent six-year period, gross weekly pay—the dollar amount written on the average paycheck—rose by about 33 per cent, but the weekly purchasing-power figure did not budge. It's not surprising that bargainers for major labor unions, if not the public at large, keep a sharp watch on the purchasing power trend. It may well be the best measure that they have of the overall living standard of the union men and women they represent.

Like all other gauges of living standards, paycheck purchasing-power statistics must be regarded with a good deal of caution. For instance, although inflation and federal income and Social Security taxes have been removed, that is all that has been removed. Government analysts haven't yet figured a way also to remove state and local levies, taxes that have risen sharply in many areas of the country in recent years. This failing suggests that purchasing-power levels would be less than the published figures if such nonfederal taxes could be taken into account.

The BLS has also not managed to take into account the so-called fringe benefits that accrue to most workers nowadays, particularly those employed by large corporations. This "nonpay pay" now runs into billions of dollars a year, and no one can pin down with certainty how many billions. How do you assign a dollar figure to a free or cut-rate round of golf at a company-owned golf club?

A recent study by the Conference Board, a nonprofit business-research organization based in New York, concluded that "a growing number of U.S. companies are liberalizing their employee benefits." The Conference Board estimated that "these benefits, including health and life insurance, retirement and disability income and severance pay, now account for 32.7 cents of every payroll dollar, up from 25.6 cents ten years ago." The study was based on a survey of 1,800 large corporations, representing a broad cross-section of U.S. business. Because larger concerns have tended to be more liberal with fringe benefits, it is possible that the Conference Board may overstate the fringe-benefit situation for the country as a whole. Even so, the findings indicate there can be little doubt that fringe benefits constitute a large and expanding element in the standard of living of many Americans, an element that is not accounted for in the purchasing power statistics.

In any event, some economists believe that if both fringe benefits and nonfederal taxes could somehow be worked into paycheck purchasing power data, the two missing elements would approximately cancel each other out. There can be no question that, at the least, they would tend to offset one another.

Another point to keep in mind about the purchasing power yardstick, of course, is that by definition it covers only employed persons. At the end of 1974, for instance, the weekly purchasing power of the average paycheck stood at about $89, some 5 per cent below the level a year before. In that same interval, however, employment declined and the unemployment rate jumped sharply, to 7.2 per cent from only 4.8 per cent a year before. Clearly, the purchasing power of the overall labor force—the jobless included—fared even worse than the purchasing power of those fortunate enough to hang onto jobs.

*   *   *

Its limited scope is perhaps the primary reason that serious business analysts attempting to gauge overall living standards usually don't rely solely on the BLS estimates of weekly purchasing power. Fortunately, broader yardsticks of our economic living standard do exist. One is a statistic produced by the Commerce Department that shows the per-capita earnings of the country's population after all tax payments—nonfederal as well as federal—have been taken into account. Like the purchasing-power series, the per-capita income series is expressed in terms of constant dollars, with inflation re-

moved. But unlike the BLS series, per-capita income figures take into account the entire population: Newborn
babies, jobless individuals, persons who never have
worked and never will, those too rich to work, and those
too poor to work. It also embraces income from all sorts
of sources besides simply the job—interest payments,
stock dividends, welfare payments, Social Security payments and the like. Indeed, it can be argued that the statistic is too wide-ranging, and that such questionable components as welfare payments are better omitted.

Not surprisingly, the per-capita income figures don't
always move the same way as the BLS series on paycheck
buying power. In 1973, for example, the income statistic
rose from a per-capita average of $2,931, expressed in
constant dollars on an annual-rate basis, to $2,952. In the
same 12 months, the purchasing-power statistic declined
from about $96 weekly, again in constant dollars, to $94
per week.

Anyone trying to ascertain whether the country's overall standard of living rose or fell during 1973 would be
hard pressed to come up with a definite answer. The per-
capita income figure, with welfare and Social Security
payments included, would indicate a rise in living standards. But the purchasing power of weekly pay would
suggest the opposite to be the case.

Perhaps the safest advice for anyone trying to gain perspective on this all-important facet of the economic scene
is: Keep an eye on both statistics. It should be added that
the dichotomous situation in 1973 was more the exception than the rule. It was a most difficult year to cat-
egorize, marked by severe inflation, an unprecedentedly
severe Arab oil squeeze late in the year, and, near the
end, a rising rate of joblessness.

Other yardsticks can also be used to gauge living standards. For instance, the BLS also issues indexes that show the buying power of hourly pay. And the Commerce Department provides data on per-capita GNP, adjusted for price changes. Neither series, however, seems as appropriate a measure of living standards as the weekly purchasing power series or the per-capita income level.

All sorts of imaginative ways to delineate the standard of living have been devised by economists from time to time. Perhaps the most intriguing—and one that can be very easily constructed without resort to the help of a professional statistician—is something called the "discomfort index." Unlike most other yardsticks discussed, but like Mr. DeVoe's CLIUI, it is not a serious economic gauge. It does help us shed light on how the nation's economy may be faring at a particular time. It is obtained simply by adding together two of the headline grabbers—the overall rate of unemployment and the rate of increase of the consumer price index.

Looking back over the years since World War II, we see that our level of "discomfort" tended to be lowest in the 1950s, during President Eisenhower's White House years. In four of the Eisenhower years, joblessness and inflation rates, added together, came to less than 6 per cent, and in two of those years the combined figure was 4 per cent or less.

In many more recent years, of course, *each* of the two rates has exceeded the 6 per cent mark.

Arthur Okun, a prominent economist who has taught at Yale and served as a top adviser to Democratic political leaders, has half-seriously picked 9 per cent as the "discomfort" level—at which the country can be said to become "quite unhappy." In some recent years, exceedingly miserable ones on the economic front, the discomfort index has registered in the 20 per cent range, more than double Mr. Okun's threshold for considerable unhappiness.

* * *

To gain increased perspective on the question of living standards, many economists have taken steps in recent years to try somehow to pin down elusive "social factors" in our standard of living. Efforts toward improving "social" yardsticks have been undertaken, among others, by the National Bureau of Economic Research, Inc., a nonprofit, private, business-research organization based in New York, with a California office as well. The NBER, of which we shall hear more later, has launched in recent years a variety of studies aimed at devising ways to measure noneconomic elements that enter into the question of living standards. A recent annual report of the bureau shows studies under way by its economists "to construct indicators of health, education, environmental quality, civil rights, public safety [and] cultural participation."

The difficulty of pinning down such imponderables can be suggested by a simple example. A recent study by the Paris-based Organization for Economic Cooperation and Development (OECD), whose members include the major industrial countries of the non-Communist world, shows that American citizens generally have more years of education under their belts than citizens of any other major country. For example, young American workers, on the average, have completed at least 12 years of school, according to the OECD study. Close behind the U.S. in this admirable regard is the United Kingdom. In fact, older Britons, with nearly 10 years of schooling, on the average, actually are slightly ahead of their American counterparts. Yet other statistics, based on such purely economic yardsticks as the real GNP, show that the U.S. and the U.K., over the years since World War II, have been among the most sluggishly advancing nations in the industrialized world. In West Germany, where the population has generally received far fewer years of schooling than in America or Britain, economic growth has been far more impressive. In terms of per-capita income, the West Germans are moving up fast on the Americans and long ago overtook the British, whose standard of living, in economic terms at least, is now one of the lowest in Europe.

But what about the relative education levels? Should the West German economic gains somehow be scaled down because their schooling appears to have been less extensive than that of the Americans or the British? And how could that possibly be done statistically? And who can say, anyhow, that seven years in West German schools is necessarily less educational and worthwhile than a dozen years in U.S. schools or ten years in British schools? Where does education fit into the picture in efforts to pinpoint living standards?

A similar imponderable is of more recent vintage. In the last several years, efforts have been undertaken in the U.S., and in other countries with highly developed economies, to curb the polluting effects of industrialization on air, water, soil, and other natural resources. To its considerable credit, the U.S. has moved more rapidly to institute various pollution control devices and techniques—in factories, on automobiles, at power plants—than any other major nation. This would appear all to the good, and obviously it has served to enhance, or at least preserve, the attractiveness of life in the U.S. In that sense, then, the country's living standards have generally benefited. However, in economic terms, more often than not the installation of pollution control equipment in factories or wherever has tended to reduce the efficiency of operations. In economic terms, productivity—a matter that will shortly be discussed in greater detail—tends to be curtailed. And this curtailment, in turn, acts to limit gains in such basic economic yardsticks as the real GNP.

The paradox is readily apparent. Without efforts to keep industrial pollution under control, our living standards—economic as well as otherwise—eventually would deteriorate horribly in the smog-filled final years of this century. But the immediate effect of such efforts is to limit gains in the only statistics that we have available to show us roughly just how high—or low—our living standards may be.

The growing American effort to curtail pollution can be put into focus with a few statistics, provided by economic researchers at Lionel Edie. In 1975, about 11 per cent of spending by U.S. manufacturers for new plants and equipment was primarily aimed at curbing pollution, rather than at expanding output, reducing costs or otherwise improving the efficiency of operations. In 1967, according to the Lionel Edie analysts, some 2 per cent of such spending was aimed at pollution abatement. Thus, the share of such outlays being devoted to the basically nonproductive purpose of preserving the environment rose about fivefold in barely eight years. Had all those antipollution dollars been poured into highly efficient new production facilities during the eight years, such economic yardsticks as the real GNP and weekly purchasing power might have made a better showing. But would our standard of living really be higher than it is today? One hardly can believe so.

**Efficiency**

It is possible, then, to measure in rough economic terms—if not in social terms as well—the country's average standard of living. Further perspective on the overall state of the country's economy can be obtained through statistics that provide insights into the all-important efficiency with which labor and production facilities are utilized. Without improving efficiency over the years, our living standards would deteriorate in short order.

The importance of an efficient labor force was emphasized recently by Herbert Bienstock, a top BLS official, in charge of the bureau's big New York office. Addressing a "Conference on Labor" in New York, Mr. Bienstock stressed repeatedly that the productivity of the labor force constitutes "the key to raising American living standards." Conversely, he added, lagging labor-force productivity is "linked to a decline in living standards."

What do we really mean when we talk of labor productivity? How can we keep track of it? Why is it, as Mr. Bienstock says, the "key" to our economic standard of living?

The image of productivity that tends to prevail in most people's minds is only half right.

Simply put, productivity is—as most people believe—the measure of what a worker can produce within a specified time. Normally, it is calculated in terms of output per man-hour, or per person-hour as women's liberationists have recently renamed the yardstick. It is the production that results from one employee working for one hour.

However, the additional public impression—that times of high productivity levels necessarily indicate a particularly energetic, hard-working labor force and that times of low productivity imply a lazy bunch of workers—is not generally correct.

The key to labor productivity in these modern times is not the energy or enthusiasm of individual workers—though these qualities do play a role—but the efficiency of the equipment that they must operate.

To illustrate, a report by Herman Nickel in the February, 1975, issue of *Fortune* magazine notes that per-worker production of automobiles at British Leyland, the big United Kingdom manufacturer, was recently running at six cars annually, while per-worker car output at a comparable Japanese automobile producer was roaring along at 35 cars per year. There is no question that the Japanese labor force has generally shown more enthusiasm toward work in recent years than most British workers, or most American workers, for that matter. Some Japanese employees, for instance, delight in group-singing special songs in praise of the corporations that employ them—hardly a likely prospect in the United Kingdom or the U.S. Still, by no stretch of the imagination can it be claimed that the typical Japanese auto production worker labors six times harder in the course of a year than his British counterpart—the legendary British tea break notwithstanding.

Relatively disharmonious labor-management relations in Britain are a part of the explanation. But the primary reason for the relatively high level of Japanese productivity—in autos and in most other Japanese businesses as well—is simply that Japanese workers have enjoyed the benefit of more modern, efficient machinery and other facilities than their British counterparts. Some fundamental statistics, compiled by the OECD, tell the story. In a recent 13-year period, Japanese spending for new machinery and other production facilities amounted to 33.4 per cent of the country's overall spending for nonmilitary purposes. In the same 13 years, output per man-hour in the Japanese labor force rose at an average rate of 10.5 per cent. In the United Kingdom, in contrast, production outlays during the 13-year period came to only 18.9 per cent of total nonmilitary spending, and, by no coincidence, the hourly output of British workers rose at an annual rate of barely 4 per cent, less than half the comparable Japanese productivity rise.

The U.S. figures are not much better, it should be noted. Of seven major countries surveyed by the OECD, only Britain spent a smaller share on new machinery and other facilities than the U.S. Of course, it can be argued that military expenditures in the U.S. gobbled up dollars that would otherwise have poured into streamlining civilian automobile plants, appliance factories and the like.

In any event, the figures leave little doubt that Japanese workers are so amazingly "productive," in large part because they are fortunate enough to be equipped with relatively modern facilities.

How can we keep track of productivity in the U.S. labor force? Quite easily, if we know where to look. Again, the BLS is our main source. Each quarter, the bureau issues two indexes showing output per man-hour in private businesses. One includes agricultural workers, the other does not. BLS statisticians compute productivity estimates using that part of the real GNP represented by private enterprise for their output estimates. This eliminates productivity "gains" really due to rising prices, and it also removes government workers, whose productivity is extremely difficult to gauge. The quarterly statistics are issued in index form, it should be noted, rather than as constant-dollar amounts. The 1967 productivity level is used as a "base" of 100. By the end of 1973, for example, productivity in private business stood at about 115; that is, the average worker's hourly output rose 15 per cent in the 1967–73 period. As it happens, that amounts to an increase of slightly under 3 per cent yearly, or close to the average annual rise in productivity in U.S. business over the post-World War II era.

Such productivity estimates, of course, must be treated as estimates only, and not taken as exact reflections of actual worker efficiency. As we have seen, the real GNP, which underlies productivity statistics, is less than an exact representation of overall economic activity. Moreover, the difficulty of precisely measuring the "output" of personnel not directly involved in turning out a product—for example, an appliance salesman at Sears, Roebuck—vastly complicates obtaining accurate estimates. This is one reason that the BLS eschews government employees in its quarterly productivity reports. How do you measure the productivity of a BLS statistician? Certainly not by the number of statistics that he can grind out each hour.

Nonetheless, BLS productivity estimates, despite their limitations, do allow us valuable insights into the overall economic situation. They are sufficiently precise to provide, for instance, a solid understanding of why, in a particular period, the country's economic living standard, on the average, may be rising or falling.

The connection that Mr. Bienstock stressed between productivity and the standard of living is fundamental. Productivity, according to Webster's dictionary, is "the ability . . . to produce." In the economic world, as we have indicated, this "ability" is normally measured in terms of the amount of goods and services that workers turn out in a given period, usually an hour. Productivity gains facilitate a "better life" for workers because they tend to increase the purchasing power of paychecks. And productivity gains are essential in stopping inflation because they tend to offset cost increases due to higher pay.

If a worker gets 10 per cent more pay per hour, but also produces 10 per cent more widgets per hour, there's nothing inflationary about his pay boost, and his standard of living tends to rise. But if he gets 10 per cent more pay and produces no more widgets than before, or perhaps even fewer, the pay boost can be highly inflationary, and very possibly will ultimately tend to reduce rather than improve his living standard. It drives up the employer's labor costs and puts the employer under pressure to offset the added expense through boosting prices, laying off personnel, or perhaps both.

There are many ways of illustrating the enormous economic importance of productivity. For example, an 0.1 per cent speed-up in this year's rate of productivity growth would add more than $1 billion to the year's GNP. Looking backward, unit labor costs in the 1960–65 period, one of nearly inflation-free economic expansion, rose only 0.4 per cent per year, on the average. But without productivity advances during those years, the average annual rise in labor costs would have topped 4 per cent. Inflation would have eaten more into living standards and the growth of employment would have been much less robust.

It is no coincidence that economic living standards have risen far more rapidly in some nations than others in recent years. The leaders invariably have been countries whose productivity gains have been such that pay boosts were largely or entirely offset—and therefore rendered noninflationary—by the rising hourly output of workers. In a recent five-year period, output per man-hour in Japan rose at an annual rate of 14.2 per cent. Average annual productivity gains of 5 per cent and more were also recorded during the same five years in such other countries as the Netherlands, Sweden, France, and West Germany. Trailing, with productivity advancing at annual rates of only 3 per cent or so, were Britain and the U.S.

In Japan, and to a lesser extent in the other high-productivity countries, the productivity gains were of such a magnitude that employers were generally able to give workers hefty pay increases each year without the increases fueling inflation or causing severe unemployment. In effect, because of their rising productivity each year, these workers' living standards were able to rise as well. In the U.K. and the U.S., where productivity gains were relatively meager during the five years, no such rise in living standards was possible.

*        *        *

An efficient labor force, then, contributes mightily to the health and growth of the overall economy. And worker efficiency, we have seen, can be approximately gauged through a perusal of readily available BLS data. In much the same manner, to gain the same sort of economic perspective, one can also gauge—with somewhat greater precision, in fact—the efficiency with which the country's production facilities, be they modern or relatively obsolete, are being utilized. This can be done by glancing at various surveys that estimate the potential capacity of production facilities in the U.S., as well as the percentage of those facilities actually being used to turn out goods at a particular time. The percentage is aptly called by economists the "capacity utilization rate," or simply the operating rate.

Perhaps the most widely followed of these surveys is one worked up monthly by the economics department of McGraw-Hill, Inc. Essentially, McGraw-Hill (which publishes a wide variety of books and business magazines) conducts confidential surveys of manufacturing concerns to find what portion of their production facilities they are using. From these periodic surveys, McGraw-Hill constructs monthly estimates of capacity utilization. The estimates provide a valuable yardstick of how efficiently—

or inefficiently—American industry may be running at a
given time.

During the post-World War II era, for instance, Mc-
Graw-Hill and similar surveys show that plant operations
in the U.S. have ranged from below 70 per cent to above
95 per cent of capacity. The records go back to 1948. The
highest rate occurred in 1951, when the Korean War
placed heavy demands on U.S. industry. The rate never
dropped below 70 per cent until the beginning of 1975, a
period of severe business distress in the U.S.

The matter of precisely where, within this rather broad
range, factory operations fall during a particular month
yields an important clue to how efficiently the overall
economy is performing. At first glance, one might suppose that periods when plant operations are very high—
above 90 per cent of capacity—are enormously prosper-
ous times, marked by an economic performance of admirable efficiency. But this, strangely, tends not always to be
the case. Economists have determined that when plant
operations reach such high levels, efficiency actually
tends to decline—production bottlenecks grow more
frequent, frustrating shortages develop, costly delays
in delivering goods to customers occur with exasperating regularity. Ultimately, costs begin to go up and profits begin to go down. Given a choice—and, of course,
the ideal figure varies considerably from industry to industry and from company to company—American manufacturers, generally, regard the area of roughly 85 per
cent as the best, or in the jargon of economists the "pre-
ferred," rate of plant operations.

*     *     *

A word should be inserted here with regard to the
question of how efficiently the country's overall economic facilities happen to be running at a particular mo-

ment. The McGraw-Hill survey, as well as most others like it, by definition is limited in scope to areas of the economy in which industrial products are involved. It does not cover facets of the nation's economic scene in which, for example, the "product" may be a service rendered. To glimpse this larger picture, government economists have devised statistical estimates of what they reckon to be the economy's potential level in terms of the real GNP, under unstrained, healthy, relatively inflation-free conditions. Economic operations during World War II, for example, would be viewed as highly strained and considerably above the so-called potential GNP level, with widespread shortages, rationing and other manifestations of an overloaded economy.

It is possible, using this concept of potential and real GNP, to see how closely the real GNP figure, discussed in the previous chapter, approximates the potential figure. It assuredly is a relationship that anyone interested in taking a closer look at overall economic performance should know about. However, the derivation of the potential GNP figure involves some highly subjective judgments on the part of the government economists, mainly the President's three-man Council of Economic Advisers, who are responsible for producing the estimate. As a result, it is questionable whether the levels of economic potential estimated by the government are reasonably close to reality. The suspicion is that the government estimates tend to err on the high side, so that larger "gaps" show up between the real and potential GNP figures than may actually exist. Without getting into technical considerations, one major reason that the economy's potential level of activity may in fact be lower than the government would have us believe entails a controversial question: What constitutes "full" employment in America? In arriv-

ing at a figure for the economy's potential real GNP—
which government analysts placed close to $950 billion in
constant-dollar terms at the start of 1976—a key assumption has been that the country's labor force is fully employed when the jobless rate is at 4 per cent; lower unemployment than that, in the official view, would contribute
to the sort of boomy, strained economic environment associated with times like World War II, when overall economic activity actually exceeds the potential level.

Traditionally, full employment has been the term that
economists apply to the ideal situation, in which joblessness is as low as it can be without triggering serious
inflation, through overburdening the country's labor resources. It may be true that years ago 4 per cent was a
nearly ideal level for efficient economic performance in
the U.S. At the end of 1965, for instance, unemployment
did in fact amount to 4 per cent of the labor force. The
consumer price index was rising very slightly at the
time—at an annual rate of less than 2 per cent—and yet
economic activity was expanding at a brisk pace.

Nowadays, however, many analysts feel that basic
changes in the makeup of the overall economy, to be discussed in detail later, make the 4 per cent figure for full
employment unrealistically low. And if 4 per cent is too
low a rate, if 5 per cent or so is a more realistic jobless
rate, then the government's idea of potential GNP begins
to look unduly sanguine. Economists of The Boston Co.,
a Massachusetts investment-research firm, worked out
what the potential GNP level would have been in 1975
had the government used 4.75 per cent instead of 4 per
cent as the full-employment rate. The Boston Co. analysts
came up with a potential GNP figure about $7 billion
below the official figure. Their estimate suggests, among
other things, that the economy in 1975 was operating

considerably closer to capacity—in effect, more efficiently, but also with less of a cushion against a reemergence of inflationary pressures—than the official record shows.

Despite its shortcomings, however, the potential GNP estimate—which is published on a quarterly basis by the Commerce Department—does allow us a fuller view of the general health of the economy. In addition, it is an important statistic to bear in mind when one attempts to ascertain the likely moves of economic policy makers in Washington. At this point, suffice it to say that, when policy makers see a widening gap developing between potential and real GNP, many of them, especially the more politically-minded, become itchy to undertake measures aimed at stimulating economic activity more vigorously.

*     *     *

There are, of course, countless additional ways in which it is possible to gain perspective on how efficiently the overall economy may be operating. One way is to examine the economic performance from a standpoint of quality, an admittedly imponderable element that can mean different things to different people. However, periodic surveys by the nonprofit Conference Board in New York and other such economic research organizations, as well as by the government, can provide an impartial, rough idea of how well the country's production and service facilities are performing.

An example is a recent survey by the Conference Board of the nation's 500 largest consumer-goods companies. The Conference Board survey found that fully a quarter of the companies polled were involved in product-recall campaigns. "It is estimated that recalls will total at least 25 million product units a year throughout the rest of this decade," the report stated, and "the actual number may be even larger, since there are thousands of unreported recalls." The survey also found that "the number of product liability suits is growing swiftly, with hundreds of thousands of grievances—real and imagined—being filed in city, state and federal courts." From a strictly economic point of view, the study went on, the rash of recalls poses some major "hazards," because the trend "could place many small and medium-sized companies in extreme financial jeopardy." The trend also indicates, of course, a rise of slipshod, inefficient work in American factories and elsewhere. It is an aspect of our economic health that simply can't be determined by merely perusing data on operating rates or the size of the GNP gap.

## As Others See Us

In a delightful poem called "To a Louse," Scotland's great 18th-century poet, Robert Burns, wrote:

> "O wad some Pow'r the giftie gie us
> To see oursels as others see us!
> It wad frae mony a blunder free us,
> And foolish notion."

The statistical yardsticks discussed so far in this book have represented ways of looking at the economy from a largely national perspective. When we look at figures that bear on the labor situation or production levels or price levels or living standards or productivity, we view the economy not in broad world terms, but in a strictly U.S. context. We can determine whether the real GNP, for example, went up or down in a given period, and how rapidly. But to gain the broadest possible perspective on the trend, whatever it may be, it would help to be able, as Robert Burns observed in pondering a very different situation, to be able to see ourselves as others see us. In our personal lives, as the poet suggested, the feat may be well-nigh impossible. But in trying to assess the nation's economy, there are ways to gain a bit of external perspective.

A brief mention has already been made of international comparisons. We have seen, for instance, that worker productivity in Japan has tended year after year to outpace productivity gains recorded in the U.S. We also have seen that it is possible to put into international perspective such matters as the share of U.S. spending that goes into new machinery and other production facilities. Other such comparisons can be made, using a wide range of economic measures, from GNP data to CPI data, available in moderately reliable form. Many of these will be discussed in a later chapter.

In addition, there are several yardsticks that can be readily used to catch a glimpse of our economy as it appears to others. Like other economic measures reviewed in this chapter, these internationally oriented yardsticks rarely command big headlines. But anyone who takes the trouble to follow them will obtain a broader view of the general health of our economy.

One such yardstick is the country's international balance of payments. As the name implies, the balance of payments is derived from the record of financial transactions that take place between the U.S. and the rest of the world during a particular period. Issued on a quarterly basis by the Commerce Department, the balance-of-payments statement covers receipts and payments involving both private and government transactions, whether settled in cash or financed by credit. It includes, for example, merchandise trade, tourist expenditures, sales of military equipment and interest and dividends deriving from international investments.

The balance-of-payments statement helps us gain a broader view of our economy because it gives us a look at America's financial standing vis-à-vis the rest of the world. If we see, for example, that the country's balance of payments in a particular quarter is in surplus, this normally suggests, in world terms, a relatively healthy U.S. economy. It indicates that, in its overall business dealings with other countries, the U.S. is managing to take in more money than it must pay out. The precise reasons for the surplus can be found in a breakdown of the Commerce Department's quarterly statement. We may find, for example, that large inflows of foreign funds occurred because goods made in the U.S. were in particularly strong demand around the world, or because many foreign investors decided that the time seemed right to plow large amounts into companies based in the U.S. In either event, the implication is that the U.S. economy is relatively attractive and healthy.

Conversely, a balance-of-payments deficit normally signifies that the country's economy is performing relatively poorly in world terms. It may be that foreign-made merchandise is winning U.S. customers away from American-made goods. It may be that foreign investors take a skeptical view of investment opportunities in the U.S. while American investors would rather put their resources into business projects abroad than at home. Whatever the case, the pattern does not inspire confidence in the condition of the U.S. economy.

A further word should perhaps be said about that part of the international balance of payments that has to do with trade. For good reason, almost as much attention is paid to the balance of trade by serious economic analysts as to the overall balance of payments.

The country's trade balance is simply the relationship between its exports and its imports. If U.S. trade with the rest of the world is in surplus, this obviously speaks well for the international competitiveness of U.S.-made goods. If a deficit occurs, it suggests that U.S. products aren't faring well in the world marketplace. Some business analysts feel that by concentrating on the country's trade balance, rather than on its overall payments balance, they can get a clearer, simpler reading of the U.S. economy's international standing. They contend that the overall payments figure can be too wide-ranging, just as we have seen that GNP estimates can be too wide-ranging. The balance-of-payments position, for example, can be affected significantly during a given quarter by flows of funds that represent merely speculative efforts to make a quick profit on interest-rate differences between the U.S. and other countries. Such "hot money" flows are hardly a true indication of the economy's basic well-being.

Trade figures, in contrast, normally offer a straightforward sign of how the country's products are stacking up against those of other countries. This is a major reason why America's trade figures are deemed far more significant than their size would lead one to expect. U.S. exports, for example, have amounted in recent years to less than 10 per cent of the country's GNP, far less than the comparable percentage in most industrialized lands.

Without going into the full record here, it is important—and disheartening—to observe that both the U.S. balance of payments and the U.S. balance of trade, though showing some strength in 1975, were extensively in deficit in many recent years, not surprisingly years that must go down as generally dismal ones for the nation's economy.

*     *     *

There is another important international yardstick that can help us to see our economy as others see it—the international value of the American dollar. At any given moment, we can readily determine how much the dollar in our pocket is worth in terms of a particular item that we may wish to purchase. All we have to do is venture into our local supermarket or clothing store to discover precisely how much our dollar can buy. But this will not tell us a great deal about the dollar's value in the rest of the world. It won't tell us what foreigners think of our dollar. We may find that our dollar can buy more food in the supermarket this week than last week because food prices have dropped; its value within the context of the local supermarket has increased. But it may be that although our dollar's buying power at the supermarket has risen during the week, its international value during the same seven days has fallen. It may buy more bread and peanuts, but it also may buy fewer Swiss francs or West German marks or Dutch guilder at banks and other business places where one country's currency may be exchanged for another's.

Many of the economic statistics that we have discussed thus far, and many of the important economic indicators that we will presently take up, are denominated in dollars, some adjusted to take the country's inflation rate into account, as we have seen, and some not adjusted for inflation. Such statistics, adjusted or unadjusted, can be assessed more meaningfully if one also is aware of how the dollar stands internationally.

Like a deficit in the balance of payments or the balance of trade, a prolonged decline in the value of the dollar in terms of other currencies normally suggests a relative weakness in America's economic situation. The reason could be, for instance, that international investors feel there are better opportunities for their funds elsewhere and therefore have little need to acquire U.S. dollars with which to buy into U.S. projects. Ultimately, the supply of dollars will tend to exceed the demand for dollars in international dealings, and the dollar's international value will tend to sink.

A glance at the important matter of productivity, for instance, helps illustrate further why it is so vital to keep the dollar's international value in mind while studying many economic statistics. As noted, productivity gains in the U.S. in a recent five-year period trailed the corresponding increases in Japan and various other industrialized nations. However, the U.S. productivity performance appears still more dismal if one takes into account the fact that the U.S. dollar's value during the period declined sharply in terms of Japanese yen and most other currencies of countries whose gains in productivity were significant. During the five years studied, as reported, the hourly output of U.S. workers rose at an average annual rate of only about 3 per cent. But the BLS bases such estimates on hourly output figures denominated in dollars; in mid-1971, for instance, bureau analysts calculate that U.S. workers in private industries produced $6.52 of goods and services hourly, after adjustment for inflation. What the BLS does not—indeed, cannot practically—take into account in its productivity figures is the international value of the dollar. During the five years in question, it was declining sharply in terms of most other major currencies.

If the BLS had recalculated its estimates of U.S. hourly output in terms of, say, yen, that 3 per cent annual rise in

U.S. productivity during the period would have evaporated. Instead, a decline in productivity would have occurred.

It obviously is too much to expect the BLS and other issuers of important economic statistics to recalculate all their dollar-denominated statistical indexes in terms of various foreign currencies. On the other hand, it is a relatively simple matter for the interested layman who wishes to gain a broader view of the U.S economy to bear in mind that there is a second way of looking at many important economic yardsticks—by viewing them against the background of how strong or how weak the dollar may be in international currency markets at the time in question.

To wit, an economy in which productivity is rising 3 per cent annually and the dollar is weak, is a much less impressive one than an economy in which productivity is rising 3 per cent annually and the dollar is strong.

# Chapter 4

## UPS AND DOWNS

A CYCLE, according to the Merriam-Webster dictionary, is "a period of time occupied by a series of events that repeat themselves regularly and in the same order."

It is necessary to appreciate something about cyclical behavior to gain a fuller understanding of what we mean when we talk about "the economy." In preceding chapters, we examined several of the more significant yardsticks that economists have devised to provide snapshots, as it were, of overall economic activity. We saw how such widely followed measures as the unemployment rate, the gross national product and the consumer price index are put together and may be used—with caution—to glimpse the general economic picture. We also examined a variety of less well-known statistics, from paycheck purchasing power to productivity to balance-of-payments data, that provide additional perspective on the state of the economy.

A fuller understanding of the economy necessitates not only a familiarity with these yardsticks. It also requires an appreciation of how the economy tends to move. Like waves in the sea or flames in the fire, the economy is in constant motion. The statistical yardsticks that we scrutinize for economic perspective are constantly changing. A fuller understanding of the economy entails an understanding of how it moves.

It is a striking sort of movement. Research extending
back over more than 120 years—well before Civil War
days—shows that the economy moves in a cyclical fashion.
In line with the dictionary definition of a cycle, the economy has tended to move in a manner that repeats itself in
an orderly sequence. This cyclical behavior can be seen in
economic record books, whether one chooses to peruse
data involving jobs or the GNP or prices or any one of
many other economic gauges.

Impressed by the cyclical nature of economic activity
over the years, economists have managed actually to pinpoint, within each economic cycle, distinct phases—alter-
nating periods of expanding and then contracting economic activity. These phases have been pinpointed down
to the precise months in which each began and ended.
Periods of expanding economic activity, appropriately,
are referred to as expansions or recoveries. Periods of
contracting activity are called, also appropriately, contractions or recessions. The end of each expansion phase is
marked by a distinct peak, as economists call it. The end
of each recession phase is marked by what economists call
a trough. The level of economic activity has risen greatly
over the years because, quite simply, the expansion
phases have been overwhelmingly longer, on the average,
than the periods of contraction.

As one might expect, the expansion periods are
marked by increases in such wide-ranging gauges as the
gross national product and by declines in such others as
the unemployment rate. Conversely, recession periods
usually witness a climb in the unemployment rate and a
drop in the gross national product after adjustment for
price changes—the real GNP, as described earlier. In
noninflationary times, it should be noted, the GNP itself,

as well as the so-called real GNP, has also tended to shrink during recessionary phases of the business cycle.

A brief review of the up-down movement of the economy over many decades should help to underline how cyclical the pattern has been.

## Records

Economists of the National Bureau of Economic Research, a nonprofit business-research organization based in New York, undertook many years ago the task of pinpointing these ups and downs of business. To determine the precise peaks and troughs, they have used—and continue to use—not only such headline-grabbing yardsticks as the GNP and the unemployment rate but scores of other statistics. Some of these others are measures already discussed in detail, such as prices and productivity. Others will be reviewed in due course. Still others, including highly arcane statistics guaranteed to befuddle and bore most laymen, and perhaps some economists as well, need not be delineated here.

The National Bureau has managed to chart this cyclical pattern of the economy all the way back to 1854, about as far back as the research organization dares to go without having to rely on statistical data whose accuracy, to put it mildly, may be questionable.

The cyclical behavior of the economy seems so well established that analysts automatically take it into account when they try to estimate the future business course. In early 1975, a time of worsening recession in America, with unemployment rapidly rising and the real GNP plunging, Albert Cox of Lionel Edie argued that better times were down the road because—simply—"the business cycle is working its way toward recovery." In other words, recessions inevitably are followed by recoveries.

Economists occasionally do come along who, out of an optimistic nature or merely ignorance of economic history, convince themselves that the economy's cyclical behavior has somehow become outdated, that healthy economic growth can be sustained indefinitely through diligent policy making and that nasty, recurrent recession periods are avoidable. In this regard, I can still recall an encounter in the mid-1960s with Otto Eckstein, a young Harvard economics professor who at that time was serving as a member of the President's Council of Economic Advisers, a panel of three economists charged with providing advice on economic policy to the country's chief executive, who then was Lyndon B. Johnson.

The encounter occurred in New York City, just after Mr. Eckstein had addressed a large conference of business executives, a well-heeled audience that seemed delighted with the economist's highly optimistic appraisal of future business developments. The overall economy at the time had indeed been expanding for several years, after a recession that ended in early 1961. Understandably, recession memories had been getting distant and dim. Some economists, including Mr. Eckstein, were beginning to talk boldly about a new era dawning in which the economic course could—and would—be made smoothly expansionary year after year after year. Recessions, to these sanguine analysts, were merely a memory from the benighted pre-1961 past.

Unconvinced, I had recently written an editorial in *The Wall Street Journal,* where I served at the time as economic news editor. Among other things, the article suggested that anyone, from President Johnson on down, who believed that the business cycle was dead and buried, and recessions with it, might be in for some rude surprises in the years ahead. The article apparently attracted the attention of Mr. Eckstein, a notably sanguine member of Mr. Johnson's economic team. Accordingly, when we happened to meet in New York, the Presidential adviser turned to me and, fixing me in his bespectacled gaze, inquired loudly: "You don't really believe that stuff you wrote the other day about a recession coming along, do you?" Rather than engage in a public debate with a high-ranking Washington official, I chose the cowardly path and, mumbling an unintelligible response, quietly removed myself from the circle of business executives who were mingling around the diminutive professor, mostly to express their admiration for his cheerful, recession-free appraisal of economic prospects.

\*     \*     \*

As both Mr. Eckstein and I now know, the business cycle lives. The expansion phase that was well under way when he gave that optimistic address in New York persisted only until 1969, when a recession set in that lasted for one year. Since then, of course, the ups and downs have kept coming. As pointed out, the National Bureau's record-keeping of these cycles, in extensive detail, begins with 1854. According to the bureau's estimates, a business-cycle trough occurred in December of that bygone year. The ensuing recovery phase continued for a full two-and-a-half years, until a business-cycle peak was reached in June, 1857. The subsequent economic contraction from this peak lasted until December, 1858, an 18-month recession. That is unusually long for a recession, according to National Bureau records. Then another up-phase in the cycle started, until a peak was reached in October, 1860. That 22-month expansion was followed by an eight-month recession, which in turn was followed by a 46-month expansion phase that encompassed the Civil War.

Altogether, the record indicates that since that first expansion phase began in December, 1854, there have been 28 expansions and an equal number of recessions. The National Bureau, whose analysts tend to be extremely cautious about such matters, generally doesn't label expansion or contraction phases of the business cycle until many months after the fact. This procedure allows the Bureau ample time to collect, scrutinize and reflect upon scores of economic statistics, some of which are slow to be compiled or subject to repeated revision. For this reason, National Bureau analysts only in 1975 came around to setting a precise trough date for the recession that ended in late 1970. The month that they finally picked was November.

A summary of the business cycles determined by the National Bureau since 1854 shows, among other things, that through 1970 the expansion phases averaged 33 months and the contraction phases 19 months. The longest expansion on record was the aforementioned 1961–69 expansion, which lasted 106 months. The second-longest expansion on record was an 80-month upturn in 1938–45. And the third-longest, somewhat strangely, was a 50-month upturn that ran from 1933 to 1937, a period of double-digit unemployment. The National Bureau's record-keeping, it should be explained, focuses strictly on whether the economy has been in an up-phase or a down-phase. Thus, one of the longest periods of economic expansion in the country's history occurred during the country's worst depression. Of course, the economy was rising from horrendous depths. The real GNP, among other key yardsticks, did not regain its pre-depression level before a new down-phase set in during 1937. The shortest expansion phase on record was a 10-month upturn in 1919–20.

As for business downturns, the longest was not the famous 1929–33 collapse; that lasted a long 43 months. The longest contraction of economic activity took place between October, 1873, and March, 1879—altogether a miserable 65 months. The shortest recession on the books lasted only seven months, in 1918–19. The next shortest, eight months long, occurred in 1945.

Both those short recessions, it should be noted, occurred in wartime. National Bureau records, in fact, give scant support to arguments that the U.S. economy needs wars to keep expanding. Five recessions, in all, have taken place partly or entirely during wartime. In addition, the records show that some of the longest periods of expansion took place in peacetime. The record-breaking 1961–69 expansion is classified as a wartime upturn by bureau analysts. However, the healthiest growth during that expansion actually transpired before the U.S. became deeply involved in military operations in Vietnam.

National Bureau data also show how the various expansions and recessions compare in terms of vigor and weakness. The length of a particular phase has not always been a useful indication of its character. For example, that extremely short slump in 1945, mentioned above, was marked by a 35.4 per cent plunge in industrial production, while a 13-month recession in 1926–27 was marked by a drop of only 7 per cent in industrial production. By the same token, the 50-month economic expansion in 1933–37 can hardly be remembered as a period of business vigor. Far more vigorous, for instance, but shorter, was the 45-month expansion of 1949–53.

\*     \*     \*

What the long record since 1854 demonstrates, through all the varying expansions and contractions, is the cyclical way in which the economy tends to expand. It is like the walker who gets to his destination ever so slowly by taking two steps forward and then one backward.

The late Wesley C. Mitchell, who headed the National Bureau in its early years, and Arthur F. Burns, the Federal Reserve Board Chairman who followed Mr. Mitchell as head of the bureau, attempted to define the cyclical nature of business in a 1946 paper. In part, they concluded, "a cycle consists of expansions occurring at about the same time in many economic activities, followed by similarly general recessions [and then] revivals which merge into the expansion phase of the next cycle."

A 1962 study by the Federal Reserve Bank of Philadelphia also stresses the cyclical nature of economic growth. The Philadelphia bank emphasizes that this cyclical behavior entails two kinds of economic growth—rapid growth during expansion phases of the business cycle, and long-term growth that accumulates over decades—in part because expansion phases are, in general, much more durable than contraction phases.

The bank puts the situation this way: "Sometimes the economy could be said to be underweight. Sometimes it is operating below its capacity and output tends to stagnate. A significant proportion of factories and machines are not in use and unemployment is high. The immediate need is to grow back to the full employment level. Although some may not think of it as such, this is desirable growth . . . because if more people go to work, there should be more goods and services produced for each person in the country to enjoy." The bank then proceeds to describe long-range economic growth: "The other kind of growth is more of a long-range thing. It could be compared to the way a child grows taller by building bone and muscle. In economic terms, we could say, it is increasing the nation's overall ability to produce."

In summary, the bank states: "Where the first kind of growth is filling out to use existing capacity, the second kind means adding to that capacity. And it also results in more output per capita because each worker becomes more efficient and is able to produce more goods and services. Both kinds of growth, of course, may happen at the same time, and it is often difficult to distinguish between them."

It is possible, using statistics with which we already are familiar, to see over the very long pull what level of growth this cyclical behavior of the economy has produced. Perhaps the best statistic for the purpose is the real GNP. Government estimates show that the real GNP in this century has grown at an annual rate of almost precisely 3 per cent per year, on the average. Growth of industrial production, another broad-gauge measure of the economy that reflects the physical output of the nation's factories, has grown somewhat faster—about 4 per cent annually—over the same span. The discrepancy can readily be explained. The industrial production yardstick, which is compiled by the Federal Reserve Board on a monthly basis, does not encompass services, which of course go into the real GNP figures. Because services have expanded less rapidly since 1900 than manufacturing industries, this has tended to hold back long-term expansion of the real GNP. A major reason that service growth has lagged, simply, is that the use of high-speed, increasingly efficient machinery is mainly of benefit to the economy's industrial sector. How do you automate a haircut? How do you speed up open-heart surgery? To put it another way, the relatively slow long-term growth of services reflects considerations unrelated to the short-term ups and downs of the business cycle.

In fact, a close inspection of how various segments of the economy normally behave during times of recession shows that services hold up relatively well. It is industrial production, with its relatively high long-term growth, that generally contracts severely during recessions. Of course, the industrial sector also generally expands extra sharply when a period of economic expansion gets under way. A prime example is the highly important, highly volatile automobile industry. In good times, the industry expands car production at a fierce pace, and when times turn bad few industries cut back output more severely or, generally, appear more distressed.

### Reasons

Thus far in this chapter, we have inspected the way in which the economy moves and, in the process, has grown. The historical research of economists at the National Bureau, in the government, and elsewhere has enabled us to look back over the decades, for more than a century, and observe the ups and downs of business activity. It has allowed us to scrutinize the dimensions of any particular business cycle with regard to all sorts of data— average number of hours worked weekly, average price of 500 leading common stocks, the dollar volume of business spending for new plants and equipment, the number of new housing units under construction, and on and on.

The plethora of statistical information is useful in dozens of ways, from enabling the interested layman simply to keep a more intelligent tab on the highly complex movement of the overall economy to permitting all sorts of investors to make all sorts of investment decisions— some wise and some not so wise—about where to put their money.

However, a question remains: Why does business exhibit this cyclical behavior? What forces underlie this up-down tendency that seems to persist—to prevail—despite the best-intentioned efforts of policy makers, men like Otto Eckstein, to guide the economy smoothly along an expansionary path?

The aforementioned study of the Philadelphia Federal Reserve Bank finds a good deal of downright mystery in this up-down pattern of business growth. Indeed, its analysis is titled "The Mystery of Economic Growth." The impetus for economic expansion in large measure derives, when all else has been analyzed, "from some inner spark," the Philadelphia bank concludes, adding that "we don't know exactly how it works and until we do, it is wise not to overlook such 'old-fashioned' things as initiative, drive, incentive, motivation, confidence, and the willingness to invest."

We still do not know completely "how it works." But there are important observations that can be made. First, the nation's economy is basically founded on a system of private enterprise that even in this day of "big government" is only guided and not rigidly controlled by federal, state, or local planners. Private planners, be they shopkeepers or the chairmen of vast corporations, can err—on occasion as disastrously as government planners sometimes err. They can make bad decisions. When things are going along well, they occasionally neglect the sort of cautionary business procedures that, paradoxically, can keep things going along well. When things are going badly, they occasionally neglect to take gutty measures that can improve the situation in the long run. In brief, business decisions, whether made in Washington or in New York City or in, say, Salisbury, Conn., are made by human beings—and human beings make mistakes.

To this essential consideration must be added the fact that our economy—like the economies of major industrial nations generally—comprises, to a very large extent, businesses that deal in manufactured goods. This list ranges from such important items as automobiles, appliances, and heavy machinery to a countless array of less significant merchandise. These goods must be fashioned in factories, using such basic materials as steel, copper, and coal. They then normally must be distributed and eventually sold to customers throughout the U.S. and abroad. If factory operations are properly geared to demand, so as not to overproduce or underproduce particular items, business generally should tend to prosper and, in the long run, expand. After all, the U.S. population continues to expand, albeit at a reduced rate. In addition, technological progress tends to bring higher worker productivity, and this too should foster faster economic growth; as we have seen in an earlier chapter, rising productivity and rising living standards generally go hand in hand.

Over very long periods, these forces—an expanding population and an increasingly productive work force—do indeed promote economic growth. Without such trends, that 3 per cent yearly increase in the real GNP this century would simply not have been possible. However, the economic decisions that underlie the production, distribution and sale of the sundry items that pervade the marketplace cannot be tailored precisely to ever-changing patterns of demand. Business planners, in other words, can never be so wise as to preclude a cyclical pattern in the movement of the economy.

\*       \*       \*

In practice, manufacturers generally do try to keep a close watch over the inventory situations of their wholesalers, who in turn generally do try to keep abreast of the inventory positions of their many retail outlets. In recent years, computers have no doubt facilitated such efforts. But mistakes continue to be made. Morris Cohen, chief economist of Schroder Naess & Thomas, a New York investment research concern, provides a reasonably typical example of how thoughtful business analysts view the role of inventory policy in the larger business-cycle picture: "While inventories represent a small fraction of the total economy, big swings in inventory changes have typically provided the main reason for business cycles."

When business is going well, business planners sooner or later make the error of overestimating the prospects for further economic gains, inventories pile up, workers must be laid off, and we wind up with a recession. When business is not going well, businessmen tend to believe that the depressed state of affairs won't ever end. It eventually does end, of course. Inventories are worked down. But businessmen, still in a recessionary mood, are slow to gear up to meet burgeoning customer needs. Eventually, they must scramble to catch up—and we get economic growth far above that long-term rate of 3 per cent. Indeed, we all too often get economic growth that is too rapid, and brings with it shortages, overstrained production and, sadly, painful inflation.

This recurring tendency to overestimate and underestimate was driven home to me many years ago, when, as a young reporter in Chicago for *The Wall Street Journal,* I was responsible, among other ignominious duties, for covering conventions that major appliance dealers held annually at Chicago's vast Merchandise Mart. My practice was to buttonhole as many dealers as possible during the two or three days available and ask them quite specifically how business was faring at their respective dealerships. After I had collected perhaps 40 or 50 such hallway interviews, I would try to put it all together into a trend-catching feature article for the paper, summarizing the state, at least at the retail level, of the U.S. appliance industry. The dealers proved to be remarkably candid with me, to the point where they would freely disclose such information as how their individual sales and profit margins compared with levels, say, a year earlier.

Reviewing my notes from such interviews, I began to notice an extraordinary pattern. In years when the appliance business had generally been good, for example, the dealers would generally tell me that business was "good." But then, ever the intrepid appliance reporter, I would press on and ask whether sales in the last few weeks or months were actually running as much ahead of rates a year before as, say, had been the case six months earlier. And more often than not, the ebullient fellow who had just informed me how "good" his business was would hesitatingly report that well, as a matter of fact, sales in the past few weeks were actually no higher than last year's comparable level, or maybe, now that you mention it, just a shade below it. And, if I pressed a bit further, more often than not I would find that the fellow's inventories, now that the matter came up, had taken an unexpected jump in the past month or so, and were appreciably higher than a year before. "No doubt a fluke" was the usual comment.

The same sort of pattern emerged, in reverse, when the dealers were interviewed after a year or so of lousy business. Invariably, the initial response would be that business was indeed "lousy." But further questioning more often than not would turn up a report that sales, while perhaps still lagging, were not lagging quite as badly as a month or two ago, and that inventories, while still excessive, were somewhat leaner than a few weeks ago.

In the end, it was a tricky undertaking to decipher

what these appliance dealers had to report. For usually their initial pronouncements about the business picture turned out, on close questioning, to be almost wholly backward-looking. And, of course, my journalistic task was to provide *Wall Street Journal* readers with an idea of what might lie ahead, rather than what lay behind, in the nation's appliance business. Complicating the job even more was the fact that the dealers tended, I noticed, to tailor their planning—buying appliances from wholesalers, expanding outlets, and so forth—to their experiences over the past year or two, rather than to recent sales and inventory developments.

I recall an especially frustrating series of interviews in early 1960. Invariably, the dealers at first would tell me—and I am certain they meant it—how great things were. But then it would develop that, yes, inventories were climbing sharply and, no, sales in the last three or four weeks actually weren't above year-earlier levels; in fact, they were dipping a little below year-earlier levels. Eventually, I produced for the paper a quite gloomy appraisal of the appliance business that bore scant resemblance to many of the general statements of optimism jotted down in my notebook. The headline, I recall, was: "Appliance Anxiety—Worried Dealers Cut Prices as Sales Lag, Inventories Pile Up."

The story, which appeared in January, 1960, proved—as things eventually turned out—worth the effort. It was among the first to suggest that the economy, which had been expanding, might be starting to turn sour. In fact, the expansion under way at the time shortly ended and a bona fide recession began in April, 1960.

Is it any wonder, I later thought, remembering the ebullience of those appliance dealers, that our economy periodically seems to get ahead of itself and winds up in a recession?

There is a footnote to the story that seems, in retrospect, worth adding. To round out the article, I telephoned a few appliance manufacturers, to supplement the views of the dealers. I found, to my astonishment, that most of the manufacturers, far from cutting back their production schedules in line with swelling inventories and slackening sales at the dealerships, were sharply expanding output. I recall, for instance, that the Gibson Refrigerator division of Hupp Corp. was setting its first-quarter production schedule for a whopping 57 per cent increase over the corresponding 1959 rate of output.

When the story appeared under the gloomy "Appliance Anxiety" headline, it caught the eye of the chief executive of one large maker of appliance parts, who also happened to be a director of Dow Jones & Co., *The Wall Street Journal's* corporate parent. He was so upset by its gloominess that he took up the matter with the head of Dow Jones. His market research people, the appliance executive told the Dow Jones head, foresaw a very good year and thought that the pessimistic tenor of that article by the young fellow out in Chicago was totally unjustified. The Dow Jones boss, to my great relief, suggested that we all sit back and let events take their course. The director never apologized to me. But why should he have? He provided me with an unforgettable illustration of how very nearsighted business planning, even in supposedly well-run, blue-chip corporations, can occasionally be.

As long as there is an appliance industry—never mind automobiles—there will be economic ups and downs.

* * *

In this chapter, I have observed that private planners do occasionally err, and the attitude of that Dow Jones director, I believe, underlines the point. The further suggestion has been made that government planners display a fallibility fully matching that of their private counterparts. A later chapter will detail the impact of Washington policy-making on the economy in general. An appreciation of the ups and downs of business, however, requires some mention at this point of the governmental role. The government, as noted, attempts to guide the economy in a manner conducive to steady, rather than erratic, expansion. The effort is mainly conducted through fiscal and monetary measures. Such measures involve government spending, taxation and, through the Federal Reserve Board, regulation of the nation's money supply. The last is a most important, but little understood, facet of the economic picture to be taken up at length later.

If the human beings who make policy efforts in Washington were wondrously wise, their policy might succeed so well that optimists like Otto Eckstein no doubt would be proved correct—the economy actually might expand, without recessionary interruptions, year after year after year. The wisdom in Washington would be sufficient to offset stupidity displayed perennially at the Merchandise Mart, in corporate board rooms, and elsewhere throughout the private economy.

But the reality of the situation is not at all like that. The economic policies formulated in Washington all too often prove not to be carefully and wisely constructed. And, as a result, they do not foster the sort of recession-free economic growth that would obviate business cycles. Indeed, a strong argument can be made that Washington's efforts in the recent past to eliminate the cyclical behavior of the economy may inadvertently have intensified the up-down tendency. It may be no coincidence that one of the sharpest recessions on record developed in the early 1970s, on the heels of a decade in which many Washington officials apparently convinced themselves that they really could place the economy along a permanent path of recession-free expansion.

Tilford Gaines, chief economist of Manufacturers Hanover Trust in New York City, has this to say about such Washington attitudes: "The middle years of the 1960s were a time when [policy-making] economists took an almost arrogant pride in their ability to control the U.S. economy. Policies were evolved . . . that led economists to believe they could 'fine-tune' our economic progress. . . . The economists' arrogance of the mid-1960s not only was unfounded but contributed to the difficulties that the economy later encountered."

Mr. Gaines suggests that there is an "apparent need for humility on the part of government officials, economists and others in their manipulation of . . . policy to steer the economy." The Manufacturers Hanover analyst concludes that "the changes in fiscal and monetary policy over the past 10 years have been intended to be economic stabilizers" but have in fact had the opposite effect.

Such criticism, it should be stressed, is by no means unique. Another critic is A. Gilbert Heebner, chief economist of Philadelphia National Bank. He echoes Mr. Gaines in his view that "our experience has been that government authorities are not skillful at regulating economic policy and that they usually overdo restraint or stimulus."

To sum up, ineptitude coupled often with arrogance in Washington has tended to exacerbate the economy's natural tendency to move in a cyclical pattern. A case in point is the performance of the Federal Reserve Board, supposedly immune from political pressures, with its seven governors appointed by the White House for 14-

year terms. The Fed has again and again failed to promote the sort of steady, moderate growth in the nation's money supply—on the order of 3 per cent to 5 per cent yearly—that many economists estimate would be appropriate for an economy with resources such as ours. Instead, Federal Reserve monetary policy has fluctuated wildly, from periods of excessive expansion, with monetary-growth rates above 10 per cent, to harshly restrictive periods in which the money supply actually has dwindled. The Federal Reserve's refusal or inability to regulate monetary growth more evenly—the explanation is not clear-cut—will be taken up more closely later. For the moment, suffice it to say that the up-down movement of the economy in general is matched, at the least, by fluctuations on the monetary front.

The efforts of the White House and Congress to control economic growth through fiscal measures—spending and taxing—seem often, like the endeavors of the Federal Reserve, to accentuate, rather than reduce, the cyclical movement of the economy. The White House and Congress tend, of course, to be far more sensitive to political pressures than the governors of the Federal Reserve Board, with their super-long terms. And popular demand has generally favored avoiding at almost any cost the widespread joblessness that prevailed during the 1930s. Accordingly, the tendency of the men who have occupied the White House since World War II and of Congress has been to support legislation producing—at least in the short run—more jobs. Usually, the job creation has entailed increased spending. The tone was set with the passage of the Employment Act of 1946, a short but to-the-point item of legislation stating, in essence, that the country's leaders should place job creation as their number one priority on the economic front.

The trouble has been that the fiscal stimulus has come in fits and starts, ill-timed, and often beyond the economy's digestive powers. It can be argued, for example, that the recession of 1969–70 was actually hastened and aggravated by efforts in the mid-1960s, led by President Johnson, to cut taxes while concurrently increasing spending, not only for the supposed domestic welfare but to pay for the intensifying war in Vietnam. The inflationary strains that subsequently developed in the economy—for example, sky-high loan rates—served to inhibit further economic growth, and in fact set in motion some of the very forces that led to an eventual recession.

The fact that much of the spending rise was for military purposes acted only to aggravate accumulating inflationary pressures. The reason, simply, is that spending dollars, say, for bombs puts more money in the hands of thousands of workers in military bomb factories. But it does not increase the supply of goods available for consumption. It does nothing to provide more washing machines or refrigerators or other such items that bomb production workers may wish to buy with money earned making bombs. The upshot is a situation in which inflationary pressures can intensify with extraordinary speed.

*     *     *

Though the cyclical nature of economic growth largely derives from the behavior of business planners in and out of Washington, there are outside factors that do, occasionally with a vengeance, influence how underlying patterns may develop. An example is the oil squeeze that the Arab countries imposed on the U.S. and other major oil-consuming countries in the fall of 1973. It is generally agreed that the U.S. economy was still in an expansion phase, which began in late 1970, when the oil squeeze developed. How much longer that expansion phase would have continued had the Arabs not cut the oil supply is a matter of conjecture. Forces already were developing in the fall of 1973—for example, an excessive accumulation of inventories in many businesses—that would surely have eventually led to an expansion peak and a subsequent phase of contracting economic activity. But there is no question that the jolting reduction in Middle Eastern oil supplies, with the long lines at gasoline stations and the occasional curtailment of production at fuel-short factories, hastened and very possibly deepened the recession.

Geoffrey Moore, the National Bureau's top expert on business-cycle patterns, estimates that the recession began in November, 1973, when Arab oil supplies were being curtailed. It is impossible to say precisely when the recession would otherwise have occurred. But the general view is sometime in 1974. My personal estimate is August, 1974, roughly the time such broad gauges of economic activity as the unemployment rate and the real GNP began weakening severely.

### And a Footnote

The ups and downs of the economy that already have been discussed and will continue to draw our main attention are not the only fluctuations detected over the years by economists. They are, for the purposes of this book, far and away the most important. However, it should be mentioned that other cyclical patterns have been observed from time to time by economic researchers. These divide, roughly, into very long ups and downs, so-called super-cycles extending over decades rather than only a few years, and very short down-phases within the larger expansion phases of a normal business cycle. These have been christened, somewhat ridiculously, growth recessions.

Neither of these phenomena seems clearly enough established, in my view, to warrant extensive discussion. Nor does either appear particularly useful in enabling us to keep a reasonably intelligent watch over the daily unfolding of major economic developments—if you will, over the headline grabbers. Still, a footnote may be in order simply to prevent possible confusion about the ups and downs of the economy staked out by the National Bureau of Economic Research.

Let us first briefly consider the super-cycle idea. There are at least several variations. These generally hold that above and beyond the normal cyclical pattern of economic growth there exist super-cycles within which the expansion and contraction phases thus far discussed represent mere ripples. Perhaps the most intriguing super-cycle concept is the so-called Kondratyev Wave. The name refers to the late Nicolai Dmitrievich Kondratyev, a Soviet economist whose major writings appeared in the mid-1920s. He subsequently was shipped off to Siberia, where he labored in salt mines for many years and finally died.

The idea behind the Kondratyev Wave rests to a considerable extent on the Soviet economist's studies of long-term price movements, particularly with respect to agricultural items. The Russian concluded from his extensive research that business activity actually takes on a rhythmic, wave-like pattern over extremely long intervals. Using price indexes and other economic yardsticks, mainly available for such relatively advanced countries as the U.S., Britain, and France, Mr. Kondratyev theorized that "super" business cycles exist. Now called the Kondratyev Wave, a super-cycle, according to the Russian's theory, extends over periods averaging roughly 50 years. One Kondratyev super-cycle transcends many "short-term" ups and downs that the National Bureau charts.

Underlying the Kondratyev Wave idea is the assumption that a very high degree of inevitability governs economic developments over many decades—that governments, for instance, can possibly delay but not entirely eliminate periods of "correction" that inevitably must follow periods in which economic growth reaches excessive rates.

The Kondratyev Wave theory can be applied to the U.S. economic record, going back at least to the late 18th century. Prices—and prosperity—increased markedly from the 1780s until just after the War of 1812, when a sharp price decline occurred. This period constituted, under Kondratyev theory, a "primary" recession within a super-cycle. Then, until about 1819, a "plateau" period persisted in which prices declined only moderately and economic activity seemed to recover somewhat. But after that a deep "secondary" slump set in. Prices and business activity declined sharply for a prolonged interval marked by high joblessness and spreading bankruptcies. The bottom did not come until the mid-1840s. Then a super-cycle expansion phase ensued, reaching a super-cycle peak around the end of the Civil War, half a century after the War of 1812.

Kondratyev theory contends that after the Civil War peak a super-cycle pattern developed remarkably similar to that after the War of 1812—a short primary recession, then a plateau until 1874, a prolonged secondary slump until 1896, and finally a span of renewed prosperity and rising prices until 1920.

The price collapse and 18-month recession that began in July, 1921, according to the Kondratyev Wave theory, marked still another primary recession within a super-cycle. The balance of the decade witnessed a plateau period. The Great Depression, until the late 1930s, marked a secondary-slump phase. A renewed expansion stage then developed, according to Kondratyev disciples, that continued into the early 1970s. The recession that hit the economy in late 1973, which turned out to be the harshest slump since the 1930s, represents still another primary recession, in the Kondratyev view. It remains to be seen what will develop on the economic front as the decade of the 1980s approaches. If Kondratyev theorists prove correct, the years just ahead should witness a relatively trouble-free plateau period and then, around the start of the next decade, alas, still another horrendous secondary slump.

Such ideas hardly add up to a sunny view of a capitalist economy. Yet, a vital part of the Kondratyev Wave idea is that the down-segments of each super-cycle serve as a sort of self-cleansing mechanism and establish a foundation from which renewed, vigorous economic growth is possible. Largely, it is this aspect that upset Stalin and led the Communist dictator to banish Mr. Kondratyev to Siberia where, according to Aleksandr I. Solzhenitsyn in *The Gulag Archipelago,* the Russian economist ended his days in "solitary confinement, became mentally ill there and died."

The *Bank Credit Analyst,* a monthly economic report of a Montreal investment advisory concern, recently noted that the Kondratyev idea has been attracting more attention of late. The explanation, it believes, is not complicated: "What has created a renaissance of Kondratyev Wave theory is, first, the intuitive feeling among a growing number of people that we have over the postwar period pretty well milked our economic system by pushing debt loads to the limit and that from here on we must deflate one way or another. Second, the commodity and whole-sale price explosion of 1973–74 bears a striking resemblance to that of 1919–20 and, interestingly enough, comes exactly when Kondratyev would have predicted."

Against such considerations, to be sure, must be weighed a variety of factors that seem to point in the other direction. The Kondratyev Wave, for example, assumes a flexibility within the economy, so that the aforementioned self-cleansing process may transpire. However, as the *Bank Credit Analyst* concedes, "wages are almost totally inflexible now, whereas they tended to fall in previous deflations" observed when Mr. Kondratyev was formulating his concepts. By the same token, the Russian could not have envisioned the extent of government intervention—often of an inflationary nature—that nowadays permeates economic affairs even in staunchly nonCommunist countries.

It can be argued, accordingly, that Kondratyev ideas are hopelessly out of date. It can also be argued, however, that the very inflexibilities that may seem to invalidate Kondratyev could, in coming years, produce inflation so ruinous that a Kondratyev-like secondary slump could develop in the inflation's wake. Whatever does develop, it is surely an interesting footnote to any study of economic growth that the controversial ideas of Stalin's Siberian prisoner are still alive. In the next chapter, we will take up how the economy has indeed been changing over the years, quite apart from the cyclical behavior already discussed.

Before proceeding to the matter of super-short cycles, it should perhaps be emphasized that the Kondratyev Wave is merely the longest of a variety of very long economic cycles, real or imagined, that various analysts have discerned poring over economic records in the U.S. and abroad. There are also, for example, so-called Kuznets cycles, named for Simon Kuznets, an economist who taught for many years at Harvard. These cycles, which seem to range up to about 25 years, or barely half as long as Kondratyev cycles, are characterized particularly by swings in construction activity. Economists who have studied evidence suggesting super-long business cycles cite many possible underlying factors. They range from wars to the effect of gold discoveries on world monetary growth to inventions to immigration trends to long-term weather trends and their impact on food production.

*     *     *

The idea of very short cycles—actually economic dips within the expansion phase of a normal business cycle—is of relatively recent vintage. Solomon Fabricant, a senior economist at the National Bureau, has attempted to pinpoint these intervals, which he calls growth recessions. He lists, for instance, as many as three such intervals between 1961 and the end of the 1960s, a period marking the longest expansion phase in the National Bureau records back to 1854.

Bona fide recessions, as noted, are characterized by actual declines for at least a half-year or so in such yardsticks as the real GNP and industrial production. Growth recessions, in contrast, are merely intervals within expansions in which the real GNP, for example, tends to rise relatively sluggishly. Like super-long cycles, these super-short growth recessions are mainly matters for debate among economists, and are not normal grist, certainly, for page-one economic news.

The growth recession idea, in any event, is responsible for at least one amusing, no doubt apocryphal, story about Mr. Fabricant. It comes from Herbert Stein, a genial economics professor who served as chairman of the President's Council of Economic Advisers under Richard Nixon. Mr. Stein, who clearly feels that there are weightier economic questions to concern business analysts than growth recessions, reports having seen Mr. Fabricant out walking a dog one evening.

"What a nice dog that is," Mr. Stein claims to have remarked.

"Why, this is no dog," Mr. Fabricant replied, according to the story. "It's my growth horse."

Whatever political considerations may underlie Mr. Stein's telling of the story—he understandably did not enjoy hearing the word "recession" in any form while he served in the White House—the point seems valid. A dog is a dog and a horse is a horse. And an expansion, it would appear, is an expansion. To begin trying to find tiny ups and downs within all the larger ones—which are difficult enough to track—seems almost as ridiculous as calling a dog a horse.

Chapter 5

# CHANGES

AN UNDERSTANDING of what we call "the economy" necessitates a familiarity with trends that in the long run can deeply alter its nature and performance.

There is, we have seen, a sameness about the manner in which general economic activity expands and contracts, expands and contracts. The up-phases have exceeded the down-phases, and so the economy has grown. In addition, during the long span of cyclical growth, significant changes have occurred in the makeup of the economy. Its internal dimensions have been changing while the economy as a whole has been expanding. An appreciation of these internal changes helps further to broaden our perspective.

The changes, slowly developing over decades, can be seen in a variety of ways from a variety of vantage points. Economic activity, as reported in the previous chapter, has been expanding over the very long pull of this century at an annual rate of about 3 per cent. But growth within the economy—within the sundry components of the gross national product—has not been even in the least. Some components of the GNP have lagged and others have spurted swiftly ahead, far more rapidly than the whole. As a result, the composition of the overall economy—the relative importance of particular facets of the GNP—is notably different nowadays from its composition 20 or 30 or 40 years ago. Understanding what has been happening provides an important insight into the economy now.

Let us begin the examination using the GNP data mentioned briefly in the second chapter. And let us focus our attention first on the remarkable transformation that has occurred with regard to the relative importance of private and governmental activity.

## Uncle's Growing Role

The statistics that go into the GNP make it possible to glimpse how the government's importance has expanded over the years. We observed in the second chapter that major components of the GNP include consumer spending, business spending, government spending of various sorts, and, small but nonetheless important, foreign trade results. We noted approximately how much each of these components contributed to the GNP—in effect, to overall economic activity in the country. We saw that the largest of these components is the category that embraces consumer spending. It accounts for something under two-thirds of the total. And we saw that government expenditures are a distant second, accounting for something under a third of the total. The breakdown leaves little doubt that the consumer remains "king" of the American economy.

However, none of this tells anything about changes that may be occurring—important, long-term trends—within the economy. GNP statistics in considerable detail are available back into the 1920s, and even a cursory glance at the record shows, above all else, the steady expansion of the government's economic role. It is a remarkable trend. In 1929, the GNP amounted to $103 billion and government expenditures totaled about $10 billion: In terms of the overall economy, government spending stood at about 10 per cent. It is occasionally assumed that the advent of World War II caused the first major expansion in the government's economic role, and that the much-publicized New Deal programs of President Franklin D. Roosevelt did little, in fact, to alter the economy's basic makeup. This is not correct. In 1940, well before Pearl Harbor, government spending was already up to $18 billion, while the GNP, at $99 billion, was actually $4 billion under the 1929 level. In terms of the GNP, government outlays in 1940 came to 18 per cent, nearly twice the 1929 level.

During World War II, of course, the government's share of the GNP soared, reaching a high of about 50 per cent in 1944. But that was an aberration that hardly helps clarify the long-term pattern. A jump to peacetime 1960 is more instructive. By then, the GNP stood at $503 billion, more than five times the prewar 1940 total. But government spending in 1960 amounted to $136 billion, nearly eight times the comparable prewar level. In terms of the GNP, government spending in 1960 came to 27 per cent.

Since 1960, the government role has continued to expand. It now approximates a third of the GNP, as noted. And the long rise, significantly, seems to transcend political divisions. The climb before World War II occurred largely in years of Democratic leadership in Washington. But the rise on to 1960 cuts across eight years of a Republican President. Recently, of course, the rise has persisted under two more Republican Presidents, both

avowed opponents of "big government." The rise has
gone on in peacetime as well as in wartime.

*       *       *

What sort of spending by the government has led the
increase? What has lagged?

In 1929, when government expenditures amounted to
about $10 billion, the bulk of that total—$7.2 billion—
represented spending not by Uncle Sam in Washington
but by state and local authorities. Such nonfederal spending traditionally has gone largely into salaries of public-
school and college teachers, policemen, firemen, garbage
men, and the like, and into school construction, mass-
transit facilities and other regional projects. In 1940, although overall government spending, at $18 billion, was
nearly twice the 1929 total, the state-local component
stood at only $8 billion, less than $1 billion higher than
11 years earlier. In 1960, with overall government
spending up to $136 billion, some eight times the 1940
level, the state-local component stood at $46 billion, less
than six times higher than in 1940. Now, overall government expenditures are approaching the $500 billion
mark, while the state-local component stands at roughly
$200 billion.

Today, the state-local component of government
spending, though vastly larger in absolute terms than
even as recently as 1960, amounts to considerably less
than half of all government outlays. In 1929, as noted,
state-local expenditures made up over 70 per cent of all
government spending.

Over the years, then, government spending has expanded far more rapidly than economic activity as a
whole. And within this fast-growing segment of the GNP,
spending by the federal government has risen even more
rapidly than spending by states, counties, cities, towns,

and other nonfederal authorities.

The GNP statistics also provide a breakdown of federal expenditures—between military outlays and other spending. In prewar 1940, the record shows, military outlays amounted to about a third of all federal spending. In 1960, it was still about a third of the total. But it has since dropped to under a fifth of the overall federal figure. Accordingly, it is clear that the sharpest expansion within the swiftly expanding federal sector has been elsewhere than in the much-criticized military arena. It has been, mainly, on the domestic front, which encompasses the broad field of social welfare. To gain a better insight into the sort of economy that has evolved over the decades of general expansion, it is worth examining the remarkable growth of this segment of federal spending more closely.

*     *     *

To appreciate what has transpired, it is useful first to become acquainted with a term that rarely makes the headlines—transfer payments. If spending by the federal government has risen far faster than any other major segment of the GNP, it is largely on account of transfer payments. They have soared.

What are they?

Simply defined, transfer payments are government transfers of money, acquired chiefly through taxation of business concerns and working people, to individuals who render no service in return for the funds received. Transfer payments include Social Security payments and other government-sponsored pension-type programs, unemployment benefits, food stamps, welfare payments, and various federal health-care and health-insurance benefits.

As recently as 1965, these governmental transfers of income from producers to nonproducers amounted to $37

billion, or about 7 per cent of wages and salaries paid out
that year to working Americans. In 1975, a scant 10 years
later, transfer payments soared past the $170 billion level,
nearly five times the 1965 total. Transfer payments approximate 25 per cent of wage and salary payments to
workers. Within a decade, if recent trends continue,
transfer payments will come to more than 50 per cent of
wage and salary income. President Gerald Ford warned
in 1975 that Americans might encounter a time in the
not-too-distant future when half the working-age population would, in effect, be working to support, through
their tax payments, the other, nonworking half. The rise
of transfer payments is obviously what the President had
in mind.

The boom in transfer payments, it should be added,
has gone on during expansion phases as well as recession
phases of the business cycle. Admittedly, 1975 was affected by a severe recession. But economic activity rose
substantially between, say, 1972 and 1973. Yet transfer
payments rose in both periods. In 1972–73, they increased from $103 billion to $118 billion, climbing from
16 per cent of the wage and salary total to 17 per cent.

The expanding role of transfer payments within the
overall economy has major ramifications. Quite apart
from obvious sociological considerations, the trend has
profound economic significance. Whether, on balance, it
represents a welcome or unwelcome economic development is a subject of great controversy. Understanding this
controversy facilitates a greater general appreciation of
the current economic situation.

An editorial in *The Wall Street Journal* in early 1975
expressed the serious misgivings of some observers about
the trend. "While the payments are of course defended
on the grounds of compassion," the editorial states, "they

are having a serious effect on the economy, by steadily breaking down the relationship between reward and effort." The article goes on to warn that "private production can no longer carry the burdens placed on it by government." The editorial concludes: "The nation has been flirting with the breaking point for a long time. . . . Present and future taxes, which have to be raised to finance government deficits, are now so high that it is more beneficial for more and more producers and workers to not work than to work."

The situation may or may not be that bleak. But there is no denying that the average worker's tax burden has increased mightily, just as transfer payments have increased mightily. This is made clear, for example, by a recent Conference Board report showing, among other things, that federal income-tax payments in a recent 10-year period jumped 170 per cent. The report also shows that tax payments eat up twice as much of the average individual's income today as they did 25 years ago. Social Security payments, a major component of transfer payments, soared nearly 300 per cent during the 10 years, the Conference Board further reports.

Evidence that transfer payments are rising even faster than taxes prompts observers who worry about the trend to stress another point. They express concern that the country's political leaders, who ultimately shape general economic policy, perennially are quick to sanction further transfer payments but always seem notably slow to sanction any tax boosts that might be needed to muster funds *for* transfer payments. This reluctance, it is argued, has been tending to make the economy more inflation-prone. When insufficient taxes are collected to cover rising government payments, the shortfall must be made up largely by increasing the nation's money supply—a move that can be accomplished through various actions of the Federal Reserve Board.

In any event, the argument runs, such increases in the money supply tend to be inflationary. They tend to drive up prices. In effect, the government prints money, which it then hands out to Social Security recipients, people on welfare and other nonworkers. But these nonworking recipients, somewhat like the people mentioned in Chapter Four who work in bomb factories, do little or nothing to increase the supply of goods and services available for consumption. It is an elementary rule of economics that prices will tend to rise along with the supply of money, when there is no concurrent rise in the available supply of things to spend the new money on.

Accordingly, it can be argued that the rise of transfer payments within the overall economy has altered the economy's nature in unfortunate ways. The rise has made the economy more prone to inflation. It has tended to limit the productivity of those who work by burdening them with disheartening tax obligations. It has given able-bodied nonworkers little incentive to bestir themselves.

Analysts who worry about the rise of transfer payments within the overall economy often cite Britain's troubled economic scene as an example of where the trend can lead. Transfer payments—and the high taxes that go along with them—may or may not be at fault in Britain. It is true, however, that Britain's economy has turned in an exceptionally feeble performance in recent years. It is also a fact that transfer payments bulk exceedingly large in the British economy. A recent breakdown shows, for instance, that Britain's "social contract"—in large part, transfer payments for health and welfare—now amounts to roughly 80 per cent of per-capita income in the country. By no coincidence, the income-tax rate in Britain runs as high as 98 per cent, a level hardly designed to spur individual incentive and hard work.

It remains to be seen whether Uncle Sam is heading down the same road as John Bull, in regard to transfer payments or economic feebleness. But some analysts, distressed by the rapid rise of transfer payments in the U.S. in recent years, fear that this may prove to be the case. If so, they foresee a U.S. economy that may perform far more sluggishly, and be subject to far worse bouts of inflation, than has heretofore happened. The cyclical pattern of growth will no doubt persist. However, with incentives to produce diminishing, the up-phases may become much weaker and down-phases, exacerbated by inflation, may prove more severe. Over the long pull, some analysts fear, economic expansion may prove much more difficult to achieve. That long-term growth rate of 3 per cent yearly, some believe, may become impossible to maintain in the years just ahead.

*   *   *

But there is another, very different side to the coin, and it also should be examined for a full appreciation of how Uncle Sam's expanding role, through transfer payments, may influence the economic picture. This side of the coin appears considerably less gloomy. It involves, essentially, the idea that transfer payments, far from hindering long-term economic growth, serve as a vital economic safeguard in recessionary times, when business activity may threaten to contract too severely. Indeed, the swelling role of transfer payments is at the heart of arguments that an economic scenario similar to or worse than the experience of the 1930s is most unlikely. Nowadays, the argument holds, a worker may be laid off, as in the 1930s, but, thanks to transfer payments, his purchasing power continues, albeit at a somewhat diminished pace.

Because there is no drastic elimination of purchasing power nowadays, it is claimed, a super-severe, snow-balling collapse of consumer demand is prevented. In brief, down-phases of the business cycle are automatically prevented from getting too deep.

This argument is put forward by an impressive array of analysts. An analysis of the long-range economic significance of transfer payments has been made, for example, by the economics department of Pittsburgh National Bank. "Increases in such payments help individuals to maintain income levels and have an important role in mitigating decreases in consumer spending," the analysis states, adding that "transfer payments expanded rapidly in every post-World War II recession—as unemployment grew, unemployment-insurance payments automatically expanded."

The Pittsburgh bank goes on to observe that Uncle Sam is by no means the sole source of such recession-fighting funds. Reviewing developments during the recession that began in late 1973, the report notes that many states changed their unemployment-insurance laws in 1974 and early 1975 to increase benefits. Some extended unemployment insurance coverage to include state employees, as well as to farm and domestic workers. Some also repealed provisions denying benefits to pregnant women. Minimum weekly benefits were increased in many states and eight now have a maximum benefit equal to two-thirds of the state-wide average weekly wage. A number of states, in addition, have repealed the one-week waiting period for receiving benefits. In several states, moreover, the first week becomes compensable after a claimant has been unemployed for a specific period. A number of states have lengthened or are about to lengthen the duration of benefit payments. "Most changes in unemployment insurance are in the direction of increasing payouts to individuals," the bank's analysis concludes.

Unemployment benefits are not the only type of transfer payments being boosted sharply. Social Security payments and medicare payments are on the list, along with others.

The bank's conclusion, it should be added, is clearly approving of the trend. "Unemployment compensation is one of the nation's built-in stabilizers," it declares. "During a period of generally falling business demand, production is curtailed by reducing hours and employment, as producers adjust to current levels of ordering. The unemployment that results from an output cutback and reduced sales produces a markedly lower level of overall personal income. Unemployment insurance payments and other transfers help to cushion the downward income effects of a decline in business activity. The cushioning effects of transfer payments by governments to persons means individuals, as a group, will have more purchasing power than otherwise. Everything else held constant, consumers will be able to spend more and the decline in business will not be as sharp or last as long as it would without the various benefit payments."

A similar view emanates from the economics department of New York's First National City Bank. "At the onset of the Depression," the bank declares, "there was very little by way of governmental machinery to provide income for the unemployed, the aged, the disabled and the dependent young. Now, income-maintenance programs, while far from ideal, mitigate suffering."

Such views of the economic impact of transfer payments clearly clash with the relatively pessimist argument that such income transfers tend to retard the economy's progress, weakening expansion periods and intensifying inflationary pressures. It is impossible to say unequivocally that one view or the other is correct.

## The Swing to Services

Other highly significant changes in the nature of the economy can be glimpsed in the GNP data. One that is far subtler than the surge of transfer payments, but no less important, involves the expanding role of services. Consumers devote a larger share of their budgets nowadays to services. And, by no coincidence, a rising fraction of the work force toils in service-type jobs.

Recent statistics show that approximately 41 cents of each dollar spent by American consumers is spent for service items—ranging from haircuts to TV repairs to electricity to rent to maid service. Indeed, spending for services in some recent years constituted the largest single segment of consumer spending—which, in turn, accounts for close to two-thirds of the GNP.

Until 1971, consumers consistently spent more on so-called nondurable goods than on services. In 1967, for example, consumer spending for services came to $204 billion, while consumer spending for nondurable items totaled $215 billion. The latter category—whose main components are food, of course, and clothing—recently climbed back to the number-one spot in consumer budgets, largely because its components also include oil and gasoline, whose prices since the Arab oil squeeze in late 1973 have soared.

Many analysts view the jump in oil and gasoline prices as something of an aberration and reckon that, over the long pull, service outlays will regain the number-one spot in consumer budgets. They note that in 1972, for instance, perhaps a year more representative of the long-term trend, service expenditures, at $311 billion, exceeded nondurable spending by about $11 billion.

Even with sharply higher oil and gasoline prices, the 41 per cent of consumer outlays devoted to services in 1975 was up from 39 per cent a decade earlier and from only 35 per cent two decades earlier. The 1975 percentage also exceeds rates prevailing just before World War II. In 1940, service spending accounted for about 36 per cent of consumer outlays.

The pit of the Great Depression marks the single period in which service outlays accounted for as large a share of consumer spending as they do these days. But unlike the recent situation, the predominance of service spending during those troubled times stemmed not from any surge in such expenditures. Rather, it reflected the fact that spending for service items—particularly such essential items as rent and health care—simply fell more slowly than spending for most goods.

The durable-goods category, whose key components are automobiles, furniture, and appliances, fell particularly sharply during the Great Depression, plunging from $9.2 billion in 1929 to a low of $3.5 billion in 1933. Obviously, in bad economic times, it is easiest to postpone the purchase of a car or refrigerator.

\*   \*   \*

Along with the swing to services in consumer budgets has come a still more dramatic swing to services on the job front. The rise in service-type jobs, of course, reflects in part the rise in spending for service items. It also reflects the spectacular ability of America's farms to turn out more food with fewer people tilling the soil—thanks largely to giant advances in the fertilizer and farm-equipment industries.

But that is only part of the explanation. Service-type jobs have proliferated in recent years within companies that are essentially manufacturing concerns. The production-line employee is still there, for instance, at the auto factory. But now, backing him up at headquarters, are many more clerical personnel than was the case years ago.

The reason isn't simply that we live in a period of expanding red-tape and paperwork—though this is a factor. We also live in a period of increasingly efficient machinery. People on the production line grow increasingly productive—unlike their colleagues pushing papers at headquarters. Productivity in service-type jobs is not so easily increased. To repeat a familiar question: How do you automate a haircut? The upshot is that service-type employment, largely impervious to the techniques of automation, has soared in relation to production-line jobs in recent years.

A few years ago, Victor R. Fuchs, a senior economist at the National Bureau of Economic Research, produced a remarkable study of this labor-force development entitled "The Service Economy." The 280-page report describes in detail the growing role that services play in the U.S. economy and suggests how this growth may shape American business in coming years. One result of the rise of services, he reports, is that the U.S. has become the first nation in history where more than half of the working population—roughly 60 per cent—is employed by organizations that provide services rather than goods. Moreover, Mr. Fuchs reports that nearly all the country's employment growth in the past three decades, since the end of World War II, has been accounted for by jobs opening up in the service area.

The implications of the swing to services, in Mr. Fuchs'

view, are broad indeed. He compares it with "the transition from an agricultural to an industrial economy, which began in England and has been repeated in most of the Western world." In some respects, the implications of the transition to a service-oriented economy are "revolutionary," the National Bureau analyst claims. One plainly economic implication, suggested in other studies of the general trend, is that services inject an element of stability into the economy. "Services cannot be stored," Mr. Fuchs writes. "Thus, this sector avoids the swings in output that result from changes in the rate at which business firms and consumers add to or diminish their inventories of goods." As the importance of services increases, the economist believes, "we can expect more stability."

*    *    *

A somewhat surprising implication of the swing to services, Mr. Fuchs claims, involves its possible long-term impact on the role of corporations. A common belief is that corporations will continue to expand and gain more power in coming years. But the emergence of an economy heavily oriented toward service industries militates against this assumption, Mr. Fuchs says. The manufacture of goods, he notes, is mostly accounted for by "large profit-seeking corporations." In the service sector, on the other hand, "firms are typically small, are usually owner-managed, and are often noncorporate. Furthermore, nonprofit operations, both public and private, account for one-third of the service sector's employment."

Mr. Fuchs cites statistics showing that the role of big corporations as employers has recently declined. "We may see an end of the myth of the dominance of the large corporation in our society," he declares. "Most people do not work and never have worked for large corporations [and] in the future the large corporation is likely to be overshadowed by the hospitals, universities, research facilities, government agencies and professional organizations that are the hallmarks of a service economy."

The rise of services, in the view of Mr. Fuchs and other prominent analysts, also presents a challenge to big labor unions. "More than half the persons employed in industry are union members," he notes, while the service sector "is only about 10 per cent unionized." As a result, he contends, "unless there are strenuous new efforts at organization, the continued growth of services may mean a decline in union influence in the United States."

Efforts have been made by labor leaders since Mr. Fuchs' analysis to organize more service-type workers. But their success seems limited.

A 1975 study by the Conference Board finds that "the rise in union membership has not kept pace with the growth in nonagricultural employment." In a recent 10-year period, the Conference Board reports, union membership—though up about 17 per cent in absolute numbers—dwindled in terms of overall employment. It fell to 26.7 per cent of the work force from 29.8 per cent. "The manufacturing sector of the economy has been and continues to serve as the foundation of the American labor movement," the report states. "Employment in this sector, however, has remained relatively stable, even though total nonagricultural employment has risen. Hence, though roughly half the manufacturing work force is organized, as a proportion of all organized labor, it declined to 42.8 per cent from 46.6 per cent" during the 10 years. The study indicates that the rise in jobs has come in the service area, where union organizing hasn't been nearly sufficient to offset the long-standing aversion of most service-type employees to joining a union.

The rise of services within the economy, clearly, has tended to reduce the percentage of the labor force that is unionized. But this does not mean that potential inflationary pressures due to labor costs have been reduced. It is a fact that unionized workers generally are able to drive a harder bargain with employers at the negotiating table than nonunion employees are able to achieve independently. But it is also true that unionized workers tend to be, as we have observed, in jobs where productivity can often be sharply increased through the use of more efficient machinery. Thus, sharp pay increases in such jobs don't necessarily mean higher labor costs—or higher prices for consumers. In many nonunion, service-type jobs, on the other hand, productivity gains are difficult, if not impossible, to achieve because such jobs often don't entail the use of machinery. The upshot is that relatively small pay boosts in such jobs can push up employers' labor costs—and ultimately what the consumer pays— more strongly than sharp pay increases won by, say, unionized workers in the highly mechanized steel industry.

In sum, productivity gains constitute a major offset to rising pay levels—and productivity gains generally come harder in service-type jobs, where unionization is relatively scarce, than in production jobs, where unionization is widespread. Accordingly, the swing to services in no way signals an easing of inflation due to labor-cost pressures. And, if unions grow more successful in signing up service workers, labor-cost pressures could sharply intensify.

## Unhappy Trends

The nature of the economy has been changing in other important—and unfortunate—ways. These other trends

may prove ephemeral, or they may become more pronounced. One such change, already briefly noted, and
painfully apparent to laymen as well as economic experts,
is that the economy seems to be getting more inflation-
prone. Over the very long pull, prices generally have
risen. Using the 1967 average as a base of 100, our old
acquaintance the consumer price index in 1974 pushed
above the 150 mark and in 1975 crossed the 170 level.
Again using 1967 as a base, the recent level amounts to
more than five times the CPI level of about 30 that prevailed in the early years of the century, before World
War I. And the recent level comes to nearly four times
the CPI figure on the eve of World War II.

The change that has been occurring on the inflation
front, however, isn't simply that prices have climbed
greatly since early in the century. It is that in relatively
recent decades the inflationary tendency has grown more
pronounced. The CPI, among other price yardsticks, has
risen far more rapidly in the last 35 years, for example,
than in the 35 years before that. Prices naturally do tend
to rise during brisk expansion phases of the business
cycle and fall in sluggish recession phases, largely in response to supply-and-demand forces. However, in recent
decades this tendency has greatly diminished. Prices generally have continued to rise most sharply around the
peak of expansion periods, but they also have tended to
keep right on rising, albeit more slowly, in recessions.
The upshot is that the long-term rise in prices has recently accelerated.

A few statistics show the emerging pattern. During
most of the 1948–49 recession, the CPI did indeed decline, and the price index dropped again in the 1953–54
recession, though less sharply. In the next post-World
War II recession, in 1957–58, the CPI dipped only

briefly, however, and it actually rose over the full course of the slump. In each of three recessions since then, moreover, the index has risen persistently and with increasing intensity. In fact, in some months of the slump that began in late 1973, the CPI climbed at double-digit annual rates. The index, at the same time, has tended to climb progressively more sharply in recent expansion phases of the cycle.

Many economists have devoted a great amount of their time trying to ascertain precisely why the economy seems to be more inflation-prone nowadays. There are, unfortunately, no easy answers, and any attempts to explain the development invariably provoke considerable debate, which typically divides along political and philosophical lines. A few reasonable observations can be made, however. One involves the relationship between money and prices. The word "inflation," according to Webster's dictionary, refers to "an increase in the volume of money and credit relative to available goods, resulting in a substantial and continuing rise in the general price level." One trouble has been, in the view of some analysts, that the volume of money and credit has indeed been rising too swiftly in recent decades—far more rapidly, in fact, than the availability of goods and, we should add, services. This concern was voiced recently by Richard T. Selden, an economics professor at the University of Virginia. Writing in a monthly economic survey published by Morgan Guaranty Trust Co., in New York, Mr. Selden states: "One causal element has accompanied every inflation the world has ever known: expansion of the money supply at a faster rate than output growth." He goes on in the article to detail at length the speedup in monetary growth—and in the price climb—in recent decades. For example, he divides a recent 16-year period into two eight-year segments, 1957–65 and 1965–73. The money supply rose 25.2 per cent between 1957 and 1965, he estimates, and 57.8 per cent between 1965 and 1973. Turning to prices, he finds that the general price level rose 13.2 per cent in 1957–65 and 42.5 per cent in the more recent period.

The professor bluntly blames the nation's monetary officials for, in effect, printing too much money and thereby causing a severe worsening of inflation. He calls this an "unfortunate 'greening' of America," of a very different sort than the widely publicized "greening" that Professor Charles Reich of Yale wrote about several years ago. Mr. Selden calls the overproduction of money the "real greening of America," and blames it not only for worsening inflation but many other economic ills.

The accelerating rise of the money supply has been accompanied, other statistics show, by an accelerating increase in the amount of credit pervading the economy— the other inflationary ingredient mentioned in Webster's definition. The climb of credit in the post-World War II era has been, to say the least, extraordinary. Just since 1970, total debt owed by all levels of government, all private corporations, other organizations and individuals has risen about 50 per cent. Total debt amounted recently to nearly two-and-a-half times the GNP. Only 25 years ago, debt came to 1.8 times the GNP. The inordinate expansion of consumer credit has been carefully tracked by John Gorman, a senior economist in the Commerce Department. A quarter of a century ago, Mr. Gorman reckons, the average American had to use about 10 per cent of his after-tax earnings to service accumulated personal debt—paying for interest charges and amortization of outstanding loans. Recently, this ratio, which Mr. Gorman calls the consumer's debt-service burden, has been close to the 25 per cent level.

Corporate debt, up more than 50 per cent in five years, has risen even more steeply than consumer debt. Arthur Burns of the Federal Reserve Board once called the drastic increase in corporate debt—with its inflationary implications—the nation's "number-one" economic worry.

Also on the rise, though less sharply, has been government debt. In the last five years, debt owed by the federal government has risen by roughly a third, and state-and-local government debt has climbed slightly faster—as New York's recent financial woes suggest. Altogether, total debt in the economy now tops the $3-trillion level. In 1960, the total was less than $1 trillion.

Another ingredient in the economy's growing susceptibility to inflation involves a consideration quite apart from the climb of money and credit. It is the proliferation of regulations, often government imposed, that generally serve, among other functions, to keep prices from dropping when normal economic forces would otherwise cause them to drop. Thomas G. Moore, a researcher at Stanford University's Hoover Institution, has compiled a list of some two dozen such governmental "barriers," as he labels them, to greater price flexibility within the economy. Some are of long standing, but others are of recent vintage. The list has been lengthening. It includes such regulations as special licensing restrictions that act to inhibit rate competition in the trucking business, capacity-limiting agreements in the airline business that have a similar price-propping effect, restrictions on rate competition between trucking concerns and railroads in certain areas, and a variety of costly subsidies paid to producers of all sorts of agricultural products.

"Government programs should be designed to lower prices and to make the economy more flexible, rather

than to create barriers" to competition, Mr. Moore declares. "Yet, a wide variety of government programs, both
legislative and administrative, have worked to raise prices
or costs."

Mr. Moore does not happen to mention other legislation and rules that allow monopoly-like power to a hand-
ful of huge, industry-wide labor unions. As Victor Fuchs
has made clear, there appear to be distinct limits to the
power and growth of unionism in an increasingly service-
oriented economy. Still, there can be no question that, in
certain key industries, union power has been on the rise
and that, as a result, accelerating wage boosts—and labor
costs—have added fuel to inflationary forces already
abuilding. Looking back over the general wage record
during recessions, it is readily apparent that in the last
several recessions hourly wage rates have kept right on
climbing, while in earlier slumps wage rates often declined—along with labor costs and, ultimately, the general
price level. Unions, even in construction and other industries troubled by relatively high joblessness, simply will
not entertain the idea of reducing wage rates in order to
open up more jobs. Wages in such industries have become, in the jargon of economists, inflexible on the
down-side—and so, it seems, have prices.

It is no coincidence that wages, in terms of the overall
economy, have assumed a larger role in recent years—or
that the role occupied by profits has dwindled. As a percentage of all types of income payments made each year
within the economy—ranging from interest on investments to rent collections—wages and other such employee compensation payments have risen in the past 20
years from about 68 per cent of the total to more than 75
per cent. Corporate profits have shrunk in the same span

from about 15 per cent of all income payments to less than 10 per cent.

\*     \*     \*

The economy's increasing susceptibility to inflation isn't the only unhappy change in recent years. The economy also appears to be more prone to unemployment, perhaps for some of the same reasons that inflation has been worsening. As reported in Chapter Two, the much-publicized unemployment rate is a somewhat misleading reflection of actual conditions within the labor force. There are serious questions about the way in which figures on the jobless rate are compiled. Moreover, as noted previously, such factors as minimum-wage laws tend to make the U.S. job picture appear relatively bleak. But none of this adequately explains the fact that, like inflation, unemployment in the U.S. has tended to grow progressively more severe.

Unemployment, like inflation, tends to respond to changes in the business cycle. The unemployment rate drops to relatively low levels around peaks of expansion phases and rises to relatively lofty levels around troughs of recessions. However, unemployment has tended, in recent decades, to improve only sluggishly during expansions and to become unexpectedly severe in recessions. In the recession that began in 1973, for instance, the unemployment rate reached the highest level—9.2 per cent of the labor force—since the bad old days of the Great Depression. In the 1969–70 recession, by comparison, joblessness never exceeded 6 per cent of the labor force. Still more noteworthy, unemployment has grown increasingly sticky in good times. In the first long expansion after World War II, in 1949–53, unemployment dropped well below 3 per cent of the labor force. In the next major expansion, in 1954–57, the rate fell below the 4 per cent mark. But in more recent expansions, it has rarely been that low. In the 1970–73 economic upturn, the rate managed only to edge below the 5 per cent level, and then but briefly.

Clearly, more is involved here than methods of statistical compilation and long-standing minimum-wage regulations. One factor, which will be discussed more fully later, is the increasing competition that American workers face from workers abroad, whose wage rates often may be below those of their U.S. counterparts. In early years after World War II, the clear superiority of American production facilities generally allowed U.S. workers, despite vastly higher pay levels, to compete with great success in the international marketplace. Now, of course, war-ravaged industries abroad have been rebuilt and streamlined. Relatively high U.S. wage levels can no longer be readily offset by more efficient U.S. production facilities. In today's highly competitive international marketplace, the highest-paid workers also may be the least secure. The same work often can be done at lower pay levels in other countries.

Another reason that unemployment has grown more stubborn involves U.S. demographic trends and the changing composition of the country's labor force. The job market in recent years has had to try to absorb sharp increases in two large segments of the population—women and teenagers. Increasingly, women who in another era might have been content to remain at home are seeking jobs. About four of every ten married women nowadays work, up from fewer than three in ten in the early postwar years. At the same time, the teenage segment of the population, for various demographic reasons, has swelled greatly over the postwar years. This, too, has caused what amounts to a sharp increase in the need for more jobs.

Minimum-wage regulations, and restrictive hiring practices dictated by some unions, tend, of course, to exacerbate this problem. In brief, the growth of the job market—indeed, the growth of the economy—hasn't quite managed to keep abreast of booming demands for jobs.

What has been happening can perhaps best be illustrated by looking again at the coin from the other side. Recent studies show that the percentage of the working-age population with jobs actually increased during recent periods of relatively high unemployment. In 1974, for example, when the unemployment rate rose from about 5 per cent of the labor force to more than 7 per cent, the percentage of the working-age population *with* jobs rose as well, from about 55 per cent to 57 per cent—which was a record high for this rarely publicized but significant statistical series.

Viewed in this way, the problem of unemployment, though undeniably serious and more worrisome than in the early postwar years, seems a good deal less dire than it occasionally is painted by union leaders and some politicians—usually ones heavily obligated to organized labor for its support at election time.

## Gauging the Impact

How has the changing makeup of the economy altered the nature of the business cycle? What is the net effect on the cyclical pattern of such long-term developments as the growing governmental role, the swing to services, the economy's increasing susceptibility to inflation, and the increasing unemployment problem?

Economists hold a wide range of opinions on these concerns. David M. Gordon, who teaches economics at the New School for Social Research in New York, has argued that the U.S. economy is strapped helplessly to a very nasty roller-coaster—the business cycle—on a ride made rough by shrinking company profits, worsening unemployment, and unmanageable inflation. In 1975, in a *New York Times Magazine* article titled "Recession Is Capitalism as Usual," Mr. Gordon concludes that "economic stability cannot endure in capitalist countries." Mr. Gordon plainly feels that the economy's cyclical behavior is a deeply worrisome facet of the economic scene, and one that he apparently believes can only be eradicated through a change in the country's economic and political systems, away from free-enterprise capitalism to a centrally run, socialistic arrangement. (A question might be raised in this regard concerning the recent British experience. That troubled country's economy has been moving sharply leftward in recent years—but, if anything, its economic woes have worsened along the way.)

Mr. Gordon's concern over the business cycle—and his eagerness to eliminate it—brings to mind a comment of a very different sort, made years ago by the late Dwight Morrow, perhaps the wisest of the J.P. Morgan partners. "The best way to get rid of business cycles would be to prove they are inevitable," the investment banker remarked. He did not add, though he well might have, that cyclical patterns can be detected in the record of any economic system, including those to the left of Britain and to the right of Uncle Sam.

Friedrich A. von Hayek, the Austrian co-winner of the 1974 Nobel prize in economics, holds a very different view of business-cycle developments from that espoused by Mr. Gordon. "It is not the market economy, or capitalist system, which is responsible" for worsening inflation and unemployment in recent business cycles, the elderly Austrian recently declared. "We have in fact been led into a frightful position," he continued. "All politicians promise that they will stop inflation and preserve full employment. But they cannot do this. And the longer they succeed in keeping up employment by continuing inflation, the greater will be the unemployment when the inflation finally comes to an end. There is no magic trick by which we can extricate ourselves from this position which we have created."

Other economists far friendlier to capitalism than David Gordon, however, also express pessimism about the way that they see the business cycle evolving in the U.S. William Wolman, an editor of *Business Week* magazine and former economist of Argus Research Corp., a New York-based investment-research concern, has warned that "there is a distinct possibility that the U.S. economy will take on stop-and-go characteristics that have hampered the British economy throughout the postwar years." Another prominent analyst, Albert T. Sommers, chief economist of New York's Conference Board, worries that in the last decade or so "business cycles have gotten wider and wider." His main fear, he says, "is the swings may get even wider, and that's something to worry about. We've got to examine our efforts to stabilize the economy. The evidence suggests that our failures are getting bigger as time passes." He adds: "The irony is we thought we had the business cycle licked as recently as ten years ago."

Perhaps—when the varying arguments have been heard—the best way to determine how much the nature of the business cycle has been affected by the long-term trends within the economy is to glance again at those records that have been painstakingly compiled by analysts at the National Bureau of Economic Research. Since economists at the National Bureau fix precise dates of cyclical peaks and troughs many months after the event, records showing the duration of specific expansion and contraction periods extend only up to the business cycle that began with the upturn of late 1970. Since then, of course, general economic activity has climbed to new highs, fallen sharply in what turned out to be the longest recession since before World War II, and then risen once again. The National Bureau data through 1970, however, is useful in gauging how the cyclical pattern has been changing over the very long run. There were 27 full-fledged business cycles between 1854 and 1970— Solomon Fabricant's "growth recessions" are not counted. The average length of the expansion phases in that 116-year span, as noted earlier, works out to 33 months and the average length of the contraction phases to 19 months. If the comparable averages only since 1919 are considered, however, the expansions get longer and the recessions shorter. Between 1919 and 1970, the average length of expansions comes to 42 months and of contractions to 15 months. The trend is still more apparent just since 1945. Between 1945 and 1970, the expansions average 49 months and the recessions only 11 months.

When the full dimensions of the most recent slump are finally pinpointed and worked into the National Bureau data, the averages for the post-World War II span obviously won't seem as encouraging. But this will not change the fact that generally, over the long term, expansions have been lengthening and contraction phases have been getting shorter.

Similar tendencies can be seen in the intensity, as well as the duration, of cyclical phases. Using our old friend the real GNP, we find that general economic activity declined an average of only 2.5 per cent during the contraction phases in 1945–70, but 7.1 per cent if the record is

al GNP has tended to rise more strongly in relatively recent
expansions.

\* \* \*

Altogether, the National Bureau records hardly convey
the sort of gloom that comes from such analysts as David
Gordon, or even Albert Sommers. The records indicate,
in fact, that the cyclical pattern has gradually grown less
volatile—which, after all, is not so remarkable a development in light of the growing importance of the government and of services. As we have seen, the most volatile
segment of the economic picture is within manufacturing,
where overproduction, inventory misjudgments, and
other errors in planning can be large factors. Those appliance dealers at the Merchandise Mart in Chicago—
with their perennially mistaken estimates of the business
outlook—again come to mind.

Unhappier changes within the economy—inflationary
pressures and persistent unemployment—obviously cannot be taken lightly. They unquestionably tend to restrict
the strength of expansion phases and make recessions
nastier. Ironically, the economy has grown more inflation-prone partly because of the growing governmental
role and the swing to services. Ironically, too, unemployment has become stickier partly because a record percentage of the working-age population has endeavored—with
unparalleled success—to seek jobs.

The business cycle has been changing, to be sure, and it
certainly will continue to change in coming years. But the
changes—thus far at least—have not been generally in di-
rections that pessimists stress. The recession-free economy envisaged back in the mid-1960s by Otto Eckstein
and others may never materialize. But the evidence indicates that the roller-coaster ride has become less hazardous than it was years ago.

Chapter 6

# THE PRECURSORS

ONE MAY say that the economy is "strong" or "weak." How strong or how weak? We have seen in earlier chapters that this can be gauged with some precision through the use of different statistical yardsticks. These include such headline-grabbing statistics as the unemployment rate, the gross national product, and the consumer price index, as well as such subtler economic measures as buying power, productivity, and the international balance of payments. They all help to define the dimensions—the strength and weakness—of overall economic activity.

In addition, we have seen that by carefully tracking the statistical record it is possible to discern and follow the highly cyclical nature of economic activity, through repeated expansion and contraction phases. We've also seen that it's possible, through a more detailed analysis of the available figures, to detect important changes that occur over many years in the nature of the economy, changes that can influence the economic course without essentially altering its cyclical behavior.

All of this is undeniably important to understanding what is meant by "the economy." But a very large question is left unanswered. The GNP and the unemployment rate, as well as most other yardsticks thus far discussed, tell us a great deal about how the economy looks at a particular moment. But they tell us next to nothing about where the economy may be going. The GNP in a given quarter may amount to such-and-such a figure, up from such-and-such the quarter before. But this does not tell us whether the GNP is likely to move higher still in the coming quarter and the quarter after that.

## No Expertise Required

Reasonable estimates of the future economic course can be made. And they require remarkably little familiarity with the arcane science of economics.

The importance of such efforts hardly needs elaboration. They are vital, of course, to any investor; clearly, the investment strategy to be followed when good times impend is not generally the strategy to be followed when a severe recession seems likely.

All sorts of planners, also, depend heavily on the shape of the economic outlook. An automobile producer, for instance, would not want to be caught short of cars if a sharp spurt in economic activity seemed just down the road. By the same token, an official in a policy-making position in Washington would presumably not want to pursue policies likely to retard business activity if a severe contraction seemed imminent.

Once one understands, in general terms, what comprises the economy, a more important, more intriguing game can begin—to try to fathom where the economy will go. This effort, as we will discover, can be undertaken in all sorts of ways. Some are highly unscientific and of questionable validity. Some involve extensive statistical analysis. Some widely followed statistics, that would seem at first glance to be useful indicators of the likely business course, are not. Some yardsticks, less widely known, have served nobly over the years as precursors of general economic activity.

Efforts to forecast the economy's direction, among other things, involve surprises. The unlikeliest matters have turned out to be, for some fortunate individuals, wonderfully prescient indicators of the economic future—"leading" indicators, as they are called in the jargon of economists.

*   *   *

One such individual is Tony Furgueson, a highly successful investment adviser based in New York City, just west of Fifth Avenue on 44th Street. The tall, outspoken investment adviser is fortunate, among other reasons, because his office window happens to overlook the windows of a certain hotel of dubious reputation. From his office perch across the street, Mr. Furgueson is able to observe with remarkable clarity, through half-pulled shades in the hotel windows, the level of (for want of a better word) economic activity in the rooms. Over the years, the investment adviser has found that the level of this particular activity has faithfully foreshadowed major turning points in the overall economy. Business in the rooms, he reports, invariably will begin to intensify several months before such broad economic measures as the real GNP and industrial production begin to turn up from a recession.

Indeed, when I first visited Mr. Furgueson at his 44th Street office in April, 1975, his first comment after the handshake was to report most cheerfully that business across the street had recently been showing signs of a pickup—a finding that I quickly confirmed through a glance out the window. At the time, several of the more conventional leading indicators that business forecasters generally follow were still pointing downward—incorrectly, as things turned out.

Mr. Furgueson has not attempted to analyze precisely why the correlation exists between activity across the street and in the overall economy. No doubt a wide range of subtle factors comes into play. For example: Is the West 44th Street area of Manhattan favored, for some reason, by visiting salesmen from business concerns whose operations happen to be in fields that tend to recover faster than most enterprises near the end of recessions? Whatever the explanation, Tony Furgueson is happy to be right where he is on 44th Street.

An even stranger leading indicator of economic activity that has proved highly accurate over the years—and doesn't require a perch on 44th Street, or anywhere else in Manhattan for that matter—involves the study of goats. I kid you not. An article on the front page of *The Wall Street Journal* in 1975 traced an inverse relationship that has apparently developed through many decades between the trend of the general economy and the country's goat population. When times begin to turn bad, it seems, people breed more goats. In 1973, not long before the 1970–73 economic expansion ended and a recession set in, some 15,000 new pure-bred goats were registered with the American Dairy Goat Association, located in Spindale, N.C. This was nearly three times the number registered in the middle years of the long 1961–69 expansion, when economic activity kept on climbing year after year, from one record to another.

As in the situation at 44th Street, no clear explanation has been given for what *The Wall Street Journal* calls "the goat index." One possibility is that milking a goat can hold down a family's milk bill. On the other hand, goat's milk often costs more at the store—if you can find any—than milk from a cow. The goat indicator remains a puzzle.

The list of unlikely leading indicators of general economic activity extends far beyond goats and goings-on at a particular Manhattan hotel. All sorts of people from time to time have come up with strange ways of divining what lies ahead for the economy. The list includes, for example, the length of women's dresses. When dresses begin to lengthen, the theory holds that economic activity will contract. When hemlines begin to climb, on the other hand, good times supposedly impend.

Again, there is no particular explanation for the relationship—and yet experience unmistakably shows that the relationship does exist. Is it simply that high spirits, in anticipation of better economic times, go with high hemlines, and low spirits, in fear of a recession, go with low hemlines? Or is there a more practical explanation—such as the need of dressmakers to conserve their supplies of material when business appears to be on the rise and to reduce their inventories when they feel that a slump is developing?

Whatever the explanation, the proliferation of pants in recent years renders this indicator less useful than it may once have been for those forecasters bold enough to rely on it.

\*        \*        \*

Nearly as surprising as the reliability of many unlikely leading indicators is the unreliability, as leading indicators, of some exceedingly well-known and widely publicized statistics. We have already observed that such broad indexes as the GNP and the unemployment rate tell little about the future direction of business activity. But other yardsticks that one might suppose would help to clarify the crystal balls of economic forecasters generally do not provide any such service.

Automobile statistics are perhaps the outstanding case in point. Few facets of the economic scene receive more faithful scrutiny in the financial press. This fascination is understandable, to be sure, in an economy as extensively tied to the motor vehicle as ours is. But the record shows, surprisingly, that the much-publicized ups and downs of the automobile business do not necessarily precede or even coincide with the ups and downs of the overall economy.

The record makes this clear. In the six months before the start of the 1960–61 recession, for example, new-car sales soared—from an annual rate of roughly four million to a rate of nearly seven million. Conversely, new-car sales dropped sharply in the six months before the 1960–61 recession ended—and the sales rate continued to decline sharply for another three months after the trough of the recession. A business forecaster who depended on trends in the automobile industry for his prognosticating would have been wrong and wrong again. He would have anticipated further economic expansion just before the 1960–61 recession, and he would have foreseen further months of economic contraction at the very time the economy was beginning to turn up.

"As important as it may be within the broad economic picture, the automobile industry is not a reliable leading indicator of business activity," says Geoffrey Moore of the National Bureau. If the auto industry constitutes any sort of indicator of the economy at all, Mr. Moore says, it would simply be as a "coincident" one—an economic gauge that generally goes up, down, or sideways along with other broad segments of business. The major coincident indicators include, among others, the GNP, the real

GNP, and industrial production. These statistical measures are classified by economists as coincident indicators almost by definition. The range of what they encompass is so great that, in fact, they *are* the overall economy.

The automobile business has reached such proportions in the U.S. that it very nearly falls into the same category. But not quite. The fortunes of the auto industry do not always coincide perfectly with those of business in general. For the economy in general, the 1957–58 recession ended in April, 1958. But the auto industry did not begin to turn around until after midyear. As noted, new-car sales continued to fall sharply for several months after the bottom of the 1960–61 recession. Again out of step, the industry kept operating at pre-recession levels for about six months into the 1969–70 economic contraction.

Altogether, the evidence makes clear that the auto industry, however important it may be to the general economic picture, does not serve, for all the attention it receives, as a meaningful indicator of what may lie ahead. Indeed, it does not always reflect even the current condition of business in general. It occasionally will move in one direction and the rest of the economy—in terms of consumer spending, the remaining 90 per cent-plus—will move in another direction.

Other economic gauges that receive considerable attention, but seem of limited use as leading indicators, include most consumer surveys periodically conducted by various economic research organizations. Probably the best known of these is a "survey of consumer attitudes," taken quarterly by the University of Michigan's Survey Research Center at Ann Arbor. A recent Michigan survey, typically, was based on hour-long personal interviews with 1,406 respondents selected from a nationwide sample of consumers. Conducted regularly since 1951, the

Michigan surveys attempt to measure, in the words of the director, Jay Schmiedeskamp, "consumer expectations and intentions to buy." The interviews, moreover, are designed "to explore reasons for changes in attitudes."

Another widely followed survey is the Conference Board's "consumer confidence index." This survey, conducted bimonthly, covers 10,000 households across the country. It focuses particularly on consumer buying plans. For example, it measures the percentage of households polled who plan to buy, say, a new car during the next six months. Such percentages are then compared with the corresponding figures two months earlier, and the "confidence index" is adjusted accordingly.

Not surprisingly, such surveys—and there are more than the two described—tend often to be viewed as harbingers of overall business. Their design certainly suggests that they would tend to signal future economic developments. Yet, strangely, experience shows that such surveys, like the auto industry, generally behave more like coincident, rather than leading, indicators.

This can be seen, among other places, in a perusal of *Business Conditions Digest,* a most useful statistical report published monthly by the Commerce Department. *BCD,* as it is often called, traces the ups and downs of scores of economic statistics in chart form back through most of the period since World War II. Superimposed on the chart lines for each statistical series are shaded areas, representing recession phases of the business cycle. As a result of this method of display, it is a relatively simple matter to glance at the ups and downs of any particular series and determine readily its usual behavior around turning points in the business cycle.

Among the measures recorded in *BCD* is the University of Michigan's quarterly survey of consumer attitudes.

From its poll, the Survey Research Center has constructed an "index of consumer sentiment," and the movement of this index is shown, through expansion and contraction phases of the general economy, in the Commerce Department publication. A glance at the chart shows, for instance, that the index was still dropping at the trough of the 1969–70 recession and was climbing sharply in the fall of 1973, near the peak of the 1970–73 expansion.

Geoffrey Moore of the National Bureau—the organization that sets the expansion and recession dates used by the Commerce Department for the shaded areas in the *BCD* charts—cautions against using the Michigan or Conference Board surveys, or others like them, as leading indicators. In fact, the Michigan survey is not classified as a cyclical indicator of any sort in *BCD*. It is listed simply as a statistical series deemed sufficiently noteworthy to be included in the publication.

In contrast, many other series traced in *BCD* are clearly labeled according to their usual business-cycle timing—leading, coincident, or lagging. The last category, as the label suggests, embraces economic indicators found to move up, down or sideways *after* general economic activity has done so.

Gardner Ackley, an economics professor who chaired the President's Council of Economic Advisers during the mid-1960s, flatly warns executives: "Don't rely too heavily on the consumer sentiment index when making marketing decisions." Geoffrey Moore cautions that the index seems "to be registering, rather than anticipating, what's happening to the rate of change in sales—that is, the rate of change in what people are buying." Mr. Moore's favorite gauge of consumer attitudes, in fact, is not a household survey of any sort. It is a relatively obscure index compiled by the Bureau of Labor Statistics. Called the quit rate, the index shows the number of people who decide to quit their jobs, as a percentage of the number employed.

"It takes a hell of a lot of confidence to quit your job," the National Bureau economist says, adding that "the quit rate is one objective measure of confidence—where somebody has to do something, take some specific action, to register his confidence."

However one may endeavor to judge consumer confidence and subsequent consumer buying intentions, one fact is clear. Anticipating the business cycle, while it may not require economic expertise, does require a familiarity with many statistical yardsticks. One must be aware, for example, that such measures as the unemployment rate and surveys of consumers' plans generally disclose only how things stand at the given moment. In addition, one should be able to recognize those yardsticks—and there are many—that have proved over the years to be reasonably reliable precursors of the economy.

Fortunately for those of us who do not reside on Manhattan's West 44th Street, or have no knowledge of the demographics of goats, there are a considerable number of generally available, bona fide leading indicators. Most are listed, clearly labeled as such, in the pages of *BCD*.

\*      \*      \*

Before taking up individual leading indicators that should be monitored by anyone who wishes to estimate the economy's likely direction, a word or two should be inserted about the origins of the main "leaders," as these indicators are often called.

Before World War I, economists at Harvard University selected several statistical series that seemed promising as economic indicators. These came to be called the Harvard ABC curves. These early yardsticks included the movement of stock prices, the dollar volume of checks drawn on bank deposits, and the rate of interest on short-term business loans. Warren Persons, a Harvard econo-mist, demonstrated that the so-called ABC curves tended to move in definite patterns related to the ups and downs of general business activity. For example, it was observed that stock prices generally tended to move ahead—to "lead"—the overall economy.

Writing in *Scientific American* in 1975, Geoffrey Moore attempted to explain the basis of the Harvard ABC curves. The three main yardsticks, or curves, he noted, "typically moved in sequence: stock prices first, bank debits next, and interest rates last." Mr. Moore went on to explain: "The economic logic of the sequence was that tight money and high interest rates led to a decline in business prospects and a drop in stock prices, which led to cutbacks in investment and a recession in business. The recession, in turn, led to easier money and lower interest rates, which eventually improved business prospects, lifted stock prices, and generated a new expansion of eco-nomic activity."

The Harvard economists managed to construct, using this small assortment of indicators, highly cyclical pat-terns of statistics. Each yardstick moved up and down like the overall economy, but not necessarily at the same time as the economy.

The ABC curves fell into disuse after 1929, in part because they failed to flash a warning about the severe economic contraction that developed late that year. One reason for this failure was that stock prices, viewed as a leading indicator among the curves, behaved instead like a coincident indicator. Stock prices turned down with, rather than ahead of, general business activity. Since

then, stock prices have unfailingly led the economy and
are once again highly regarded as a harbinger of overall
business. Analysts believe that their failure to perform as
a leading indicator in 1929 may have stemmed from the
severity of that stock-market plunge, one of the sharpest
on record. It was so sharp that, rather than signaling
deep trouble ahead for the economy, it had a direct, immediate impact, actually *causing* deep trouble by wiping
out savings and destroying the buying power and confidence of families at virtually all economic levels.

During the 1930s, various economists continued trying
to refine the art of forecasting through the use of statistical indicators. Extensive research was undertaken at the
National Bureau in New York. Its economists studied the
cyclical behavior of dozens of statistics. In late 1937,
Henry Morgenthau Jr., President Franklin D. Roosevelt's
Secretary of the Treasury, asked the nonprofit research
organization to devise for the government a standardized
set of indicators that would help Washington's policy
makers ascertain more accurately where the economy
seemed headed. The request grew out of a deep frustra-
tion at the White House over the fact that the economy,
after finally pulling out of the disastrous 1929–33 contraction phase and staging a recovery, once again was
beginning to nose downward.

Under the direction of the late Wesley C. Mitchell,
aided by Arthur Burns, later to become chairman of the
Federal Reserve Board, the National Bureau late in 1937
gave Mr. Morgenthau an approved list of indicators. It
included not only leading indicators but coincident and
lagging indicators as well. Used in tandem, the last two
categories are also of value in forecasting the business
course. The National Bureau list was first published, with
Washington's seal of approval, in May, 1938.

In the four decades since then, the list has been revised four times—in 1950, 1960, 1966, and 1975. The revisions were made each time to take into account new statistics, made available by more extensive surveys and by the use of computers in compiling statistical material. The revisions also reflected periodic efforts to allow for important changes in the makeup of the economy, such as those discussed in Chapter Five. The revision in 1975, for example, attempted to allow more fully for the economy's increasing susceptibility to inflation. It was found in late 1973, just before the recession began, that many leading indicators, which should have been flashing red and dropping, instead were climbing, falsely suggesting fair economic weather ahead. The indicators involved mainly were denominated in dollars—not in so-called constant dollars, which go into the real GNP, but in unadjusted "current" dollars, the kind in our wallets that are eroded by inflation.

The 1975 revision of the indicators attempted, among other things, to remove some—but not all—statistical series that can be pushed up simply by rising prices. Not surprisingly, indicators that have survived through the various revisions since 1937 tend to be ones not expressed in simple dollar terms. An example is the length of the average workweek in industry. When it gets longer, this suggests a rising level of business activity several months down the road. When it shortens, declining economic activity is indicated.

Presently, we will take up in detail the key indicators included in the latest revision. For the moment, suffice it to say that analysts have broadly segregated the many statistical series that appear in *BCD* into a few major categories—those involving jobs, those related to production, those involving investment and inventories, those

concerned with prices, costs and profits, and those involving that most basic of economic matters—money. Because
money is such an important precursor of general economic developments, and also is so often misunderstood,
it is well worth our while to take a close look at this particular leading indicator.

## Money

Money is the change in your pocket. But it takes other
forms as well. Some are readily recognizable, others are
not.

Money, essentially, is a tool. It serves a function—to facilitate exchanges of goods and services. Any medium of
exchange that provides this function, in effect, is money.
Through the ages, all sorts of items, not normally
thought of as such, have served as money. The list ranges
from stones, used in some primitive societies, to ciga-
rettes, used in war-ravaged countries in supposedly so-
phisticated modern times.

Gold, particularly, has been used through the centuries
as money, though it does not serve—officially at least—as
money in the U.S. today. The yellow metal constitutes a
highly tangible medium of exchange, and it possesses
other important monetary qualities. The value of a piece
of gold varies, of course, according to its size and purity.
Because it can be so precisely valued, gold can serve also
as a standard of exchange. In a particular business transaction, the amount and quality of gold involved can be
tailored exactly to the importance of the transaction. In
addition, because it is one of the most enduring products
known, it can serve as a store of value. It does not fade or
erode over the years. Paper money, obviously, boasts no
such qualities. Moreover, the long-term value of paper

money can easily diminish—as a result of the basic forces of supply and demand—if too much of it is printed. This has not been a problem with gold, which must be laboriously dug out of the ground and refined at great expense.

Today, in the U.S., two kinds of money are predominantly used. The first we have noted—the coins and paper bills in the pockets and purses of the public. The second kind of money, which is far more significant, is that held in checking accounts in commercial banks. Economists call this second, predominant form of money "demand deposits." They are, as the name implies, deposits that must be paid on the demand of depositors. We know this form of money as, simply, our checking accounts.

When economists talk—or more likely argue with one another—about the role of "money" in the economy, they normally are talking about these two forms of money—currency in the pockets of the public and demand deposits. Together, these two forms of money comprise what economists in their textbooks call M-1. Demand deposits comprise more than three-quarters of M-1. When we read in newspapers that the nation's money supply during a particular month or quarter or year grew at such-and-such a percentage, the money supply in question usually is M-1.

*     *     *

Anyone attempting to anticipate the general course of the economy should try to keep abreast of M-1. This involves not only keeping a tab on the pertinent statistics, which are issued weekly by the Federal Reserve and show precisely where M-1 stands each week. It also necessitates a familiarity with ways in which the movement of M-1 can be anticipated. And this requires a brief discussion of how money—that is, M-1—is created in the U.S.

First, however, it should be observed that M-1 is by no means the only way that economists define the nation's money supply. Besides M-1, there are M-2, M-3, M-4, M-5, M-6 and M-7. Without going into elaborate detail, suffice it to say that, generally, the higher the number of the particular "M," the more comprehensive it is.

As we have seen, M-1 comprises currency and demand deposits. M-2 embraces these two categories, plus so-called time deposits, which are, simply, savings-type deposits left with commercial banks over periods of time. Unlike demand deposits, they bear interest. When we get all the way up to M-7, the list includes everything in M-1 and M-2, plus deposits in savings-and-loan associations and mutual savings banks, savings bonds, shares in credit unions, and short-term, interest-bearing securities issued by the federal government, such as Treasury bills, or by corporations, such as commercial paper.

To anticipate the movement of general business activity, it is important to follow the movement, at the least, of M-1. Experience shows that the overall economy tends to follow the path of the money supply, with a lag of several months or more. The Federal Reserve reports M-1's exact total and recent movement normally every Thursday afternoon. The details appear Fridays in such newspapers as *The Wall Street Journal* and *The New York Times*. A supplementary statistical report on monetary developments is issued weekly by the Federal Reserve System's regional bank in St. Louis, one of a dozen such regional outposts of the Washington-based central-bank system. The St. Louis Federal Reserve Bank will mail its report, which contains elaborate analytic detail about monetary trends, to individuals who wish to receive it.

It also is possible to gain valuable insights into the likely

movement of the money supply. This requires an understanding of how money is created in the U.S. That process is supervised by the Federal Reserve Board in Washington and the so-called Federal Open Market
Committee. The Federal Reserve Board is made up of
seven governors, as noted earlier, each appointed by the
President for 14-year terms. The Federal Open Market
Committee is composed of the seven governors of the Reserve Board, plus five presidents of regional Federal Reserve banks. The FOMC, as it is commonly known, meets
in Washington at the Federal Reserve Building on Constitution Avenue, which also houses the Reserve Board, its
seven governors, and a large staff of economists and statisticians.

The Federal Reserve System, through the Reserve
Board and the FOMC, controls the country's money
supply mainly in three ways. The Reserve Board sets the
level of so-called reserve requirements that banks must
keep on hand, rather than lend. The banks are required
by the Board to keep on hand, in the form of cash, a
specified percentage of their demand deposits. This has
the effect of limiting the amount of lending that banks
can safely undertake. The higher the level of reserve
requirements, the more restricted becomes bank lending.

When banks lend, this tends to expand the nation's
money supply, through what economists call a "multiplier" effect. As money is lent, deposited in other banks,
and lent again—and as this process is repeated again and
again—the demand-deposit component of the money
supply obviously will rise sharply. It is possible, through
mathematics, to determine the theoretical limit of this
multiplier effect. The particular limit will depend on
where the Reserve Board sets the percentage for reserves
required to be set aside. If banks are instructed, for ex-

ample, to maintain cash reserves of 15 per cent against
their demand deposits, the theoretical limit of the multiplier effect for an original $1,000 demand deposit works
out to $6,667. This happens because diminishing frac-
tions of the original $1,000 are lent and re-lent through
the banking system. This arrangement is called a "frac-
tional-reserve" type of banking system.

No such multiplier process, it should be noted, applies
to currency in circulation, the other component of M-1.
Accordingly, an increase in the currency component of
M-1 normally will have less economic impact than an increase in the demand-deposit component, where the multiplier effect is involved.

Monetary expansion is also controlled through what is
called the discount rate. When they need funds for loans
or other purposes, private banks, as members of the Federal Reserve System, may borrow from regional Federal
Reserve banks. The discount rate is the interest charged
by the regional banks on such loans. Like an increase in
reserve requirements, an increase in the discount rate
tends eventually to restrict monetary expansion. Conversely, a reduction in the discount rate, like a reduction
in reserve requirements, tends to foster growth of the
money supply.

The third major way in which the money supply is controlled involves the Federal Open Market Committee.
The FOMC meets in Washington once or twice a month.
At the start of each meeting, Federal Reserve economists
give the FOMC a report on economic conditions in the
country and abroad, as the Fed analysts picture the situation. Later in the meeting, the 12 FOMC members vote
on what sort of monetary policy should be pursued until
the next meeting. The FOMC issues a "directive" that is
given to an official of the Federal Reserve System's main

regional bank in New York City. This official is the manager of operations of the New York Fed's so-called Open
Market Account. In accordance with his instructions from
the FOMC, he attempts to direct the operations of the
Open Market Account in such a way as to carry out as
nearly as possible the particular monetary policy sought
by the FOMC.

Through the New York bank's Open Market Account,
the manager is empowered to buy or sell, for the Federal
Reserve System, government securities in dealings with
private concerns that make a market in such issues. If the
FOMC has directed him, for example, to manage the
Open Market Account with an eye to fostering a more expansionary monetary policy, he will normally order increased purchases of securities by the Open Market Account. This buying tends to pump money from the
Federal Reserve System into the private economy, as the
New York Fed pays private sellers for securities it buys.
Conversely, when a more restrictive monetary policy is
desired, the Open Market Account normally moves to sell
government securities. This tends to pull money out of
the private economy into Federal Reserve coffers.

Many economists feel that this third method of regulating monetary growth is far and away the most potent
means available to policy makers. A 47-page booklet
called "Open Market Operations," published by the New
York Federal Reserve Bank, explains that when the Federal Reserve, for instance, "buys securities in the open
market, it creates bank reserves which did not exist before." The Fed makes payments simply by crediting the
amount of its purchase to the account of the particular
commercial bank involved in the transaction. As a result,
money is created. The booklet goes on to note that this
money-creating power derives from the Congress, which

is given the authority under the U.S. Constitution (Article I, Section 8) to "coin money [and] regulate the value thereof."

It is a simple matter to pinpoint this money-creating process by the Federal Reserve. At the start of 1975, for example, Fed reports show that M-1 totaled about $280 billion. The bulk of that—roughly $215 billion—was made up by demand deposits, with currency in circulation accounting for the rest. At the same time, M-2 amounted to about $700 billion. The far larger total, of course, reflects the inclusion of time deposits.

Over the years, as a result of Federal Reserve policies— intentional and otherwise—M-1 has grown unevenly. In the decade to mid-1965, a period that covers two recessions, M-1 grew at an average yearly rate of 2.2 per cent. In the next decade, this growth accelerated to more than 5 per cent yearly.

*     *     *

There is considerable debate among economists over just how fast the money supply should grow. A large group, led by Milton Friedman of the University of Chicago, has long argued that the monetary growth rate should be consistent with the economy's own, natural ability to grow—in effect, the rate at which the real GNP can be expected to expand in accordance with the country's resources of labor, material and technical know-how. A figure often mentioned by Mr. Friedman and others is roughly 3 per cent annually. If the growth of M-1 exceeds that level over prolonged periods, as it has done in many recent years, this will act to push the economy forward too strongly and drive up prices, Friedmanite economists contend. They blame much of the inflation and subsequent economic stagnation in recent years—the term often applied is "stagflation"—on excessive monetary expansion.

On the other hand, these same analysts warn that monetary growth considerably below the 3 per cent level over prolonged periods, or actual reductions in the money supply, will tend to restrict economic activity severely and eventually bring on widespread price cutting. This is precisely what happened, Friedmanites claim, between 1929 and 1933, a period in which the money supply contracted by about a third. A far different, expansionary monetary policy, they argue, would have largely prevented the severity of the economic contraction that developed. These economists, who obviously lay great emphasis on the importance of monetary policy within the overall economic picture, also stress that the Federal Reserve should avoid sharp monetary swings—swings from very high rates of monetary growth to actual shrinkages of the money supply. Such a roller-coaster policy, it is argued, serves only to make the economy's already cyclical behavior more pronounced and more hazardous.

In fact, possibly because the Friedmanite advice is difficult for policy makers to follow for a variety of practical reasons, monetary growth has been anything but moderate and steady. And, however annoying this unevenness may be to Mr. Friedman and his disciples, it does provide an important forecasting tool for anyone trying to figure out the future course of the economy.

*     *     *

One place where monetary developments can be readily followed—somewhat more leisurely than by scrutinizing the weekly reports of the Federal Reserve—is in the Commerce Department's monthly publication *Business Conditions Digest*. Among leading indicators listed there are several gauges of the money supply. These include changes in M-1, M-2, and M-3, which encompasses a wider range of time deposits than M-2. The indicators take the form of percentage changes occurring monthly in the various categories of money. The various changes are expressed on an annual-rate basis—for instance, an actual change of 1 per cent in a month is expressed as approximately 12 per cent—and no dollar amounts are listed.

A glance at the pertinent charts in *BCD* shows that over the years these monetary indicators have correctly, promptly signaled major turning points in the overall economy. The chart for M-1, for example, shows that this particular leading indicator has correctly foreshadowed every major recession and every expansion phase of the economy in the last 25 years—which is about as far back as the chart goes.

Not only that: The record shows that the M-1 indicator has done so earlier than most other leading indicators. Indeed, some analysts might argue that the M-1 indicator has occasionally led general business activity by intervals that are almost too long. Prior to the long 1961–69 economic expansion, the indicator began pointing upward slightly before the 1960–61 recession, admittedly a mild one, was even under way. This is not to say that the indicator failed to warn of the 1960–61 recession, as well as to signal the subsequent 1961–69 expansion. (It began warning of the recession as early as the beginning of 1959, about a year-and-a-half before the slump actually set in.)

A parenthetical footnote should be inserted here, to underline the value of the money supply as a precursor of economic movement. The 1929–33 economic contraction came as a great surprise and shock to most forecasters. As noted, the stock market, a leading indicator, for once gave no warning. However, anyone following

money-supply trends—had that been possible then—
would have begun growing cautious about the economic
outlook as far back as 1928, when monetary expansion
started to flatten out. Unfortunately, regular reports providing detailed monetary statistics were not available in
1928 and 1929. The statistics, which we have in considerable detail for those years now, showing the contraction
of the money supply in 1929–33, have largely been reconstructed by Milton Friedman and Anna Schwartz, a National Bureau economist, through a painstaking perusal
of old bank records and other such data.

Mention also should be made of the problem that inflation poses for anyone attempting to gauge the economic
outlook solely by the movement, say, of M-1. Rising
prices tend to diminish the amount of stimulation that a
given increase in the money supply will impart to the
economy. If prices rise 10 per cent and the money supply
also rises 10 per cent, "real" monetary expansion, in the
jargon of economists, is reduced to zero. In such circumstances, a 10 per cent increase in the money supply would
actually be less indicative of future growth in business activity than, for instance, a 5 per cent money-supply increase at a time when prices are rising only 2 per cent. In
the latter situation, real money-supply growth amounts to
3 per cent.

In recent years, it has become increasingly necessary to
take developments on the price front into account when
one examines monetary indicators. To illustrate: The rate
of growth in M-1 began to slow in late 1972, about a year
before the advent of the severe 1973–75 recession. However, M-1 did continue to expand before the recession hit
in late 1973. That growth, viewed in isolation, without
regard to the price picture, gave scant indication of the

severity of the recession to come.

The 1972–73 behavior of M-1 was in contrast to its behavior before recessions earlier in the post-World War II era, when inflation was not a major economic worry. For several months before the 1960–61 recession, for instance, M-1 actually declined. No such decline was evident in 1972–73. However, in real terms, allowing for rising prices, the money supply indeed did decline before and during much of the 1973–75 recession. The forecaster who viewed M-1 in these terms during 1972–73 would have had a much clearer warning of the approach and magnitude of the recession than persons who monitored only M-1, without taking the steep price increases into account.

There are extreme circumstances, to be sure, when following real money-supply trends can be misleading. One occurred during the Great Depression. As mentioned, the money supply shrank sharply between 1929 and 1933. But the economic contraction itself was so severe that prices collapsed along with the money supply. In fact, prices for a while fell even faster than the money supply. An economist visiting from Mars, examining the money-supply statistics in real terms, would have seen a moderate rise in the figures. And, from this, he might reasonably have concluded that a period of rising economic activity was unfolding. He would, of course, have been dead wrong. A disastrous decline in economic activity was in fact under way.

Nonetheless, under normal circumstances, the trend of the money supply, expressed in real terms after adjustment for price changes, constitutes a most important leading indicator. Indeed, its importance has recently become more widely recognized. The 1975 changes in the key leading indicators contained in *BCD* include the introduction of a new statistical series—the money supply, expressed in terms of the 1967 value of the dollar.

* * *

The decisions reached at FOMC meetings are not made public until many weeks afterward. This secrecy, policy makers claim, is necessary to prevent, among other things, private speculators from possibly profiting in transactions involving securities traded by the New York Fed's Open Market Account. Some critics of the Federal Reserve contend that this secrecy on the part of the FOMC is unwarranted. Whether it is or not, there are other ways to anticipate money-supply trends, besides trying to develop a pipeline into the deliberations of the FOMC. One way is simply to observe the actions of the New York Fed. These are publicly reported weekly, along with the money-supply statistics, usually on Thursday afternoons. The reports show, along with other such activities, Federal Reserve purchases or sales of government securities during the preceding week. These figures can provide an idea of Federal Reserve intentions, regardless of what may actually have happened to the money supply itself during the week.

Such weekly data, however, can prove confusing. Due to special factors that often arise, the long-run intentions of the FOMC tend to be obscured in the weekly statistics. Anyone depending too heavily on such reports from week to week runs the same sort of risk as the proverbial fellow who fails to see the forest because he has been too busy concentrating on the trees.

A better way to anticipate monetary trends is to try to analyze the sort of thinking likely to prevail among monetary policy makers at a given time. This is not as difficult an undertaking as it may at first glance appear. The ability to mind-read is decidedly not a requirement.

Few policy makers would argue strongly with Mr. Friedman's idea that in the U.S., over the long run, M-1 should rise at an annual rate of about 3 per cent, approximately in line with the economy's ability to grow. In practice, however, policy makers rarely seem free to get down seriously to the business of gearing money-supply growth to the prescribed long-run rate. Rather, they invariably become preoccupied with immediate concerns, such as whether the money supply appears adequate to prevent a spiraling of interest rates, or whether it is growing sufficiently to enable the overall economy to pull out of a recession, or, at the other extreme, whether it is growing slowly enough to prevent overstimulation and inflationary strains during an expansionary phase of the business cycle.

Further complicating the task of the money-supply managers is something that Mr. Friedman, in his call for steady, moderate monetary growth over the years, may tend to overlook–the huge budget deficits so frequently run up by elected politicians—in Congress and in the White House—who understandably find spending money far easier than raising it from taxpayers, who also happen to be voters.

Budget deficits occur, of course, when the federal government spends more than it takes in. This process naturally acts to drive up interest rates. The government—specifically, the Treasury Department—is normally compelled to borrow funds in order to make up the financial shortage.

This borrowing can occur in different ways. The Treasury can compete for money in the so-called open market, attempting to divert investors' funds that might otherwise be lent, say, to a private corporation also in need of money. This competition naturally tends to force up interest rates. More borrowers compete for funds in the marketplace, and in the process interest rates begin to climb.

However, the Federal Reserve also can purchase government securities, as we have seen. The money managers at the Fed may fear that the Treasury's borrowing needs are of such magnitude at a particular time that interest rates in the open market may climb too sharply for the general health of business. The Fed officials, in such circumstances, could decide to buy some or all of the securities that the Treasury is attempting to sell to raise money to meet the budget deficit.

The phrase that economists apply to this process is "monetizing the debt." It is an appropriate description. The upshot of such action is to create new money in the economy. The procedure may relieve interest-rate pressures for the moment. But in the longer run, such pressures may develop anyway—because increases in the money supply ultimately serve to push up interest rates. This is because excessive money-supply increases lead eventually to higher prices, and, if lenders fear rising prices, they will logically seek higher rates of interest on what they lend, in order to protect the long-term value of their loans.

Such considerations, however, are unlikely to take precedence, in the deliberations of monetary policy makers, over considerations that involve the immediate health of the economy. Time and again, the exigencies of the current economic situation have proved decisive in policy moves. This attitude may be unfortunate for the long-term health of the economy. But it enables observers far removed from the Washington scene to estimate the likely monetary course to be pursued at a particular moment. One may simply examine the economic situation confronting, say, the FOMC before one of its meetings, and then deduce the probable way in which the policy makers will react to it.

Some general assumptions can be made, and one certainly need not be a financial expert to make them. If a large deficit looms in the federal budget at a time when interest rates generally are at high levels—above 8 per cent, for example, on the bonds of the best-known, most prestigious corporations—the likelihood is that monetary authorities will provide considerable assistance to the Treasury in financing the budget debt. And, as a result, the money supply is likely to expand substantially.

On the other hand, if the federal budget is approximately in balance or in surplus—a rarity in recent decades—there will be no particular need, as economists put it, to monetize the debt. Policy makers will more likely pursue only moderate monetary expansion, in line with the long-term growth potential of the economy.

Another important consideration is the amount of inflation in the economy. If inflation is nonexistent or mild—again, rare nowadays—policy makers will doubtless feel freer to pursue monetary expansion than if inflation is a severe, worsening problem.

It's worth noting that a dilemma can develop for the authorities when the desire to prevent an interest-rate spiral in the short run runs into the desire to curb inflation. In the long run, as explained, high interest rates go hand in hand with high rates of price increase. In recent years, the dilemma has usually been resolved so as to prevent spiraling interest rates in the short run. As interest rates rise and funds become more and more difficult for borrowers to obtain, a point is reached where concern develops at the Federal Reserve over the financial viability of beleaguered borrowers. Whenever this point approaches, the money managers—ever mindful of the disastrous experience of 1929–33—invariably seem to relent in their long-term inflation-fighting and open the monetary spigot to prevent spreading bankruptcies in the short run. Despite persistent inflation, for example, the Federal Reserve eased monetary policy dramatically after the Penn Central became strapped in 1970, and took similar action after the Franklin National Bank ran into financial trouble in 1974.

A final point should be made about the behavior of the monetary authorities. As the 1973–75 recession showed, they tend not to be especially sensitive to unemployment figures. Monetary policy, which had been growing more restrictive in a battle against worsening inflation, did not clearly begin to ease until late in 1974. By then, the jobless rate had been rising for about a year. This seeming indifference to unemployment no doubt reflects the fact that, unlike Congressmen, and the President who appoints them to their 14-year terms, the Fed governors are not elected officials. To some degree, therefore, they are insulated from attack by, say, angry labor leaders. At the same time, however, as managers of the country's money and banking system, they do exhibit considerable concern, as we have seen, if trouble brews on the financial front.

It is possible, then, to gauge with reasonable precision the way in which the monetary authorities are likely at a given time to decide policy. Prevailing economic conditions will almost certainly determine whether a speedup in the growth of the money supply is likely, or perhaps a slowdown, or perhaps simply a continuation of existing policy.

*     *     *

A word of warning is necessary here. Monetary officials are not always able to produce precisely the results they deem most suitable. It is possible, for example, that the FOMC may order the New York Fed to conduct its open-market securities operations in such a way as to step up the growth of M-1 from, say, 2 per cent annually to 7 per cent annually. Through the procedures previously discussed, new money can be pumped into the banking system, through newly created demand deposits at commercial banks. However, it is possible that business demand for loans may prove to be lagging—that the new money will not be lent and re-lent as swiftly as the authorities might have anticipated. This could tend to hold actual expansion of the demand-deposit component of M-1 far below the potential, desired growth theoretically possible through the aforementioned multiplier phenomenon. In such a situation, economists would say that the "velocity"—or rate of turnover—of the money supply is lagging.

Some economists—mainly those associated with the views of Milton Friedman—believe that the Federal Reserve, if it makes the proper effort, can indeed control the growth of the money supply with great accuracy. But other economists—especially many who profess to emphasize the ideas of the late British economist, John Maynard Keynes—question whether monetary officials can in fact control money-supply growth with such precision. Indeed, many Keynesian-school economists question the entire Friedmanite notion that the trend of the money supply is central to the general condition of the economy. The Keynesians stress the importance of governmental spending and taxing—rather than monetary policy—in determining economic developments.

The questioning of the Federal Reserve's ability to exercise exact control over the expansion of the money supply undoubtedly contains some validity. But the record gives scant support to any argument that the course of money supply and the course of the overall economy are unrelated. Not only are the two clearly intertwined, but they are intertwined in such a way that money-supply trends foreshadow—by at least several months, and often longer—trends in overall business.

## Stocks

When economists of the Commerce Department and the National Bureau worked to revise and improve the list of leading indicators in 1975, in the process they assigned a rating to each indicator, much as a teacher assigns a mark between 100 and zero to students. Considerations used to determine each indicator's mark included such factors as timing, economic significance, and prompt availability. The 12 leading indicators were assigned marks ranging from a low of 69 to a top mark of 80. The bottom grade went to a relatively obscure yardstick titled, mysteriously, "vendor performance." Briefly, it measures the speed with which goods are delivered to customers. The index keeps track of the percentage of companies reporting slower deliveries each month. A rising percentage signifies a future rise in overall economic activity, and a drop in the percentage suggests a coming economic slowdown.

The two monetary yardsticks on the list of 12, reflecting monthly changes in M-1 and M-7, fared better. The M-1 indicator received a mark of 79 and the M-7 indicator received a 75. Both were judged to provide especially early signals of future changes in the economic direction. The M-1 yardstick, on the average, has foreshadowed recessions by 10 months and recovery periods by eight months. The M-7 gauge has signaled both recessions and expansions by about half a year.

The indicator that achieved the top mark of 80 is far less obscure than the vendor-performance measure and far less complicated than the money-supply gauges. The top mark went to the stock market. The precise measure of share prices used is a broad index compiled by Standard & Poor's Corp. It measures overall changes in the prices of 500 major common stocks. The more widely publicized and older stock-market index, the Dow Jones industrial average, is not listed among the key leading indicators contained in *Business Conditions Digest* because it is based on only 30 stocks. Over the years, however, its movement has closely paralleled that of Standard & Poor's index of 500 stocks.

The stock market is by no means new to the list of key leading indicators. It has survived through the various revisions of the leading-indicator list back to 1937 because, again and again, it has provided early notice of coming changes in overall economic activity. On the average, it has turned down nine months before recession periods set in and turned up four months before economic recoveries. The money supply has usually given slightly longer signals, but no leading indicator, the money-supply gauges included, is so promptly available. Indeed, if one chooses to follow the actual stock-market tape that emanates from the floor of the New York Stock Exchange, with its ticker symbols and price information, changes in individual share prices may be scrutinized on a minute-by-minute basis.

*     *     *

The high standing of the stock market as a leading economic indicator may seem surprising to many readers. A volatile economic measure, the stock market has occasionally been ridiculed as a misleading—rather than a leading—indicator. Prominent among its critics is M.I.T.'s Paul Samuelson, who several years ago commented that "the stock market has correctly predicted nine out of the last five recessions."

Julius Shiskin of the Bureau of Labor Statistics, an authority (along with Geoffrey Moore of the National Bureau) on the subject of leading indicators, sharply disagrees with such criticism: "Despite some support for Professor Samuelson's apparent view that the market is nothing but a collection of random events—a view held by many on Wall Street—I believe the evidence to the contrary is persuasive." The Standard & Poor's stock index, Mr. Shiskin goes on, "is one of the best-known and most valuable of all economic indicators; investors use it to form first impressions of the tide of their own market activities and business economists use it widely as an indicator of prospective business-cycle developments." A similar view comes from Albert Cox of Lionel Edie. "Stock prices have proven to be a highly accurate leading indicator of the business cycle over more than 100 years of recorded experience," the Edie economist declares.

Underlying the stock market's outstanding performance as an indicator of the future course of the economy is its complex relationship to other facets of the economic scene. One such link is its relationship to the profits of the corporation whose shares are constantly being traded by investors. Mr. Shiskin explains this relationship this way: "Say that it becomes known that a company is likely to earn less or perhaps lose money in the quarters ahead. Many people will offer the stock for sale, and the market price for that stock is likely to decline. The declines will tend to be spread . . . as the prospects [for reduced earnings] for various companies become known. Both an interaction and a cumulative downward effect on the stock price index is likely to take place. The decline in aggregate profits can be expected to result in a decline in new investment and still later in a decline in production and employment."

The main reason that corporate profits themselves are no longer among the key leading indicators listed in *Business Conditions Digest*—they were removed during the 1975 revision—is that, unlike the stock market, profit figures are exceedingly slow to be published. They are compiled quarterly, rather than monthly, and by the time the Commerce Department comes up with the totals each quarter, any change in the economy that may have been signaled may already be under way. Also, of course, they are dollar-denominated and therefore easily distorted by inflation.

Another relationship that no doubt underlies the stock market's ability to presage economic developments so well involves interest rates. Securities that offer fixed rates of interest compete for investors' dollars with common stocks, which offer dividends that may be increased or reduced according to changes in a company's profitability and other corporate developments. When interest rates rise, as they are apt to do when business activity begins to expand too rapidly and generates increased inflationary pressures, such interest-paying securities as corporate bonds tend naturally to become more attractive to investors. Accordingly, money is more likely to flow into the bond market than into the stock market. Conversely, when a recession approaches bottom, demand for loans usually tumbles. This decline in loan demand tends to reduce interest rates and renders interest-paying securities less attractive. In the process, the stock market becomes more enticing to investors.

A 1975 study by Argus Research Corp., the New York investment advisory service, examined the remarkable performance of the stock market as a precursor of economic recoveries. Titled "The Market As a Barometer," the Argus study concluded that the market's ability to foreshadow an economic upturn "is not the result of investor clairvoyance." Rather, the report goes on, "it occurs in response to easing financial conditions which, in turn, are largely responsible for the recovery that subsequently ensues."

\*     \*     \*

The day-to-day behavior of the stock market, to be sure, is not entirely rooted in such fundamental factors as interest-rate and profit trends. Geoffrey Moore of the National Bureau observes that "a wide variety of factors play upon the market—shifts in investor confidence, fears of inflation, prospects for higher taxes or stiffer government regulation, changes in margin requirements [which limit the amounts that investors may borrow to buy stocks], the flow of funds from abroad, a strike in a major industry, the failure of a large enterprise." Such factors, Mr. Moore believes, "make the underlying regularities [in the movement of the stock market] more difficult to observe and predict." Indeed, Mr. Samuelson's criticism that the stock market has forecast nine of the last five recessions is not without a modicum of justification. The Standard & Poor's stock index, as well as other such indexes, has occasionally dropped sharply during periods of prolonged economic expansion, before resuming a long-term climb.

\*     \*     \*

Before moving along to some other important leading indicators, it should perhaps be noted also that an investor who appreciates the stock market's close relationship with the ups and downs of the business cycle can profit greatly by this understanding. The stock market, as we have seen, can tell us the likely future direction of business. Using the same sort of analysis, it is possible to gauge the likely direction of the stock market. If one is able to ascertain with reasonable certainty the probable direction of the economy, one can make some guesses about the likely direction of the stock market. For example, if other leading indicators, such as the money supply, strongly suggest that a recession lies six months or so down the road, it is a fair guess that share prices will be moving progressively lower, if indeed a decline has not already set in. On the other hand, a general rise in key leading indicators during a recession should suggest to investors that a long-term stock-market rise is on the way.

A stock-market analysis by Raymond DeVoe of Spencer Trask, issued on March 31, 1975, provided an instance in which attention should have been paid to the stock market's relationship to the business cycle—but, unfortunately, was not. Mr. DeVoe likened his feeling about stock-market prospects at that time to the instinctive feeling that skin divers occasionally experience when a large shark is nearby. There is an ominous stillness in the water. The clear message of his analysis was for investors to be wary of the stock market and be ready, in effect, to get out of the water fast.

At the time that the analysis appeared, the Dow Jones industrial average stood at about 750. A month later, the average was above the 800 mark, and within six weeks of Mr. DeVoe's warning it crossed the 850 level. Investors who depended on their instincts on March 31 may or may not have succeeded in catching the sharp rise in share prices. It would depend whether their intuition agreed with Mr. DeVoe's that a large shark was nearby. However, investors wise enough to have kept their focus firmly on such key leading indicators as the money supply and building permits for new private housing units, another of the 12 listed in *Business Conditions Digest*, would more than likely have shaken off any instinctive fears about sharks in the water. Those leading indicators, as well as others, had been on the rise since the start of the year.

It should be added that the gains to be made in the stock market during recessions, just before the overall economy has begun to expand, can be enormous—and the economy most certainly was in a recession in March, 1975. In the final five months of the 1969–70 recession, the Dow Jones average jumped 25.8 per cent. In the first 12 months of the subsequent 1970–73 economic expansion, by comparison, the stock average rose only 4.6 per cent. Similarly, in the last four months of the 1960–61 recession, the stock index rose 16.9 per cent, while in the next 12 months, when business activity was expanding, the average rose only 6.1 per cent. A most dramatic rise in share prices during a postwar recession occurred in the last five months of the 1953–54 slump. The Dow Jones average climbed 37.1 per cent during that short period. The increase in the next 12 months, though a substantial 33.6 per cent, still fell short of the rise during the recession.

The message that emerges, clearly, is that the investor who waits until a recession is safely over before jumping into the stock market, while he may not miss the boat entirely, certainly misses the chance for a cabin in the first-class section.

## The Big Picture

Anyone attempting to estimate the likely direction of overall business activity, quite obviously, can learn a lot simply by keeping abreast of money-supply trends and stock-market figures. Indeed, there is a temptation here to advise readers to remain glued to the ups and downs of those two leading indicators—and do no more. There is even a temptation to say that the stock market alone— easy to follow, widely publicized, and remarkably accurate in its foreshadowing of business-cycle changes—can signal the likely economic course sufficiently well to enable anyone's crystal ball to function clearly.

The temptation should be resisted. "Why do we need other leading indicators? Why isn't the index of stock prices enough?" asks Mr. Shiskin of the Bureau of Labor Statistics. He proceeds to answer his own question: "Experience has taught us that there is no single, fully reliable leading indicator, and that an average of many— such as the index of leading indicators—is better than one." He cites an instance, noted earlier, of the danger involved in depending on just one or two leading indicators. The single time in the past half century when the stock market failed utterly to give early notice of a major change in the direction of the business cycle was 1929. Share prices continued merrily upward in 1929—all the way into the teeth of what turned out to be the severest economic slump in the country's history.

The money supply, like the stock market, occasionally fails as a leading indicator. In addition, the Federal Reserve is in the habit of revising its monetary statistics months after they are originally reported. As a result of such tardy revisions, the monetary picture can suddenly assume a very different shape from what it first seemed. What appears to be a period of rapid growth in the money supply, for example, can turn out, after the Fed makes a revision or two in its statistics, to be only a tiny uptick, or possibly even a time of monetary contraction.

The wisest procedure, accordingly, is to follow—if not

religiously every month, at least with reasonable regularity—a limited selection of other leading indicators that have also proved exceptionally reliable over the years.

\*     \*     \*

Considerable attention should be paid to the Commerce Department's composite index of 12 leading indicators. The 12 are selected from many dozens followed by National Bureau analysts. As noted, the makeup of the composite index was changed in 1975, the most recent in a long sequence of attempts to improve its usefulness.

The index has turned down, on the average, some nine months before recession periods and turned up four months ahead of the start of expansion phases. The 12 component indicators include, as mentioned, the stock market, the two monetary measures involving M-1 and M-7, and the vendor-performance yardstick. The other leading indicators deemed by Commerce Department and National Bureau analysts worthy of the select list cover a diverse range. Like those already named, the other leading indicators also have been assigned marks between 100 and zero. All are available monthly in *Business Conditions Digest*.

The remaining eight, with their assigned marks, include the length of the average workweek in manufacturing industries, with a mark of 73; the rate of worker layoffs in manufacturing industries, inverted, with a mark of 76; the volume of new orders for consumer goods, with a 74; new businesses being formed, with a 73; contracts and orders for new plants and equipment, with a 72; new building permits for private housing units, with a 76; changes in business inventories on hand and on order, 71; and changes in prices of raw materials used in industrial processing, 72.

A major goal of the analysts who revised the composite

index in 1975 was to remove any distortion that could creep in on account of inflation. This was a problem in 1973, when some of the key leading indicators continued to climb long after the economy, stripped of "growth" due merely to rising prices, had moved from an expansion phase to a period of contraction. The indicators that proved to be misleading, rather than leading, were mainly ones denominated in dollars—current dollars, as economists call them, the kind that you have in your wallet. Among these current-dollar indicators were corporate profits, contracts and orders for new plants and equipment, changes in business inventories, and new orders for durable goods. All were either removed from the composite index of leading indicators in the 1975 revision, or adjusted so as to be stated in terms of so-called constant dollars, which eliminates distortion due to price changes.

By the change, National Bureau economists hope to avoid a repetition of the 1973 experience. At that time, the composite index—distorted by its current-dollar components—flashed no warning of the coming recession. It did not begin turning down until mid-1974, more than a half year after the start of the most severe business slump since before World War II. Government statisticians have reconstructed the revised composite index, first published in 1975, all the way back to 1948. Significantly, with its constant-dollar indicators, the new index started to warn of the approaching recession as early as July, 1973, four months before the slump materialized.

It is clear that the use of constant-dollar indicators marks a major improvement in the composite index. A word of caution, however, should be given. In extreme economic situations—far more extreme than anything encountered in recent decades in the U.S.—constant-dollar statistics can behave strangely. It was noted in the second section of this chapter that the constant-dollar money supply—among the new indicators making up the revised composite index—actually rose for a time during the worst of the Great Depression. This was because prices were falling even faster than the money supply was shrinking. In an entirely different but equally extreme situation—Germany's runaway inflation in the early 1920s—the German money supply, adjusted for rising prices, contracted. The contraction occurred despite a flooding of the German economy with marks. Normally, such a contraction of a country's "real" money supply would signal a business slump, with rising unemployment and extensive idle plant capacity. These things eventually did occur—but later, after the inflationary bubble was punctured by German authorities at the end of 1923. Earlier, unemployment dropped toward zero and factory operations were at a high level.

\* \* \*

Any discussion of leading indicators would be incomplete without mentioning one other way in which it is possible to gain particularly early clues about the future course of the economy, especially before a downturn in business activity. We have observed that, besides leading indicators, economists have also assembled groups of "coincident" indicators, which move up or down coincidentally with overall business, as well as groups of "lagging" indicators, which tend to lag behind the broad economic trend. *Business Conditions Digest* contains composite indexes made up of selected indicators from these two categories, just as it contains a composite index of key leading indicators. The individual coincident and lagging indicators also appear in the monthly publication. Some are well-known—such coincident indicators as the GNP and industrial production, and such lagging indicators as interest rates charged by banks and labor costs.

Taken individually, neither the coincident indicators nor the lagging indicators are particularly useful in providing early hints of future turns in the business cycle. However, Geoffrey Moore of the National Bureau has found that the two sets of indicators, used in tandem, combine to make a remarkably long-leading and reliable precursor of overall business. Specifically, Mr. Moore has constructed a ratio of the two composite indexes. It is a ratio of the coincident composite index to the lagging composite index.

The National Bureau economist has estimated that the ratio of the two composite indexes has begun to drop, on the average, about 13 months before recessions have set in. This lead is appreciably longer than the average warning given by the more widely known composite index of leading indicators. The ratio of the two indexes has been less useful—but still has been valuable—signaling expansion periods. It has started to climb, on the average, about four months before economic recovery periods.

Mr. Moore is not at all surprised that the coincident-to-lagging ratio has so consistently presaged the movement of the economy as a whole. He explains that during a period of economic expansion, for instance, the ratio provides forecasters with a measure of how rapidly, in relation to general business activity, lagging indicators are climbing. These lagging indicators generally represent facets of the economic scene that by their nature tend to inhibit further growth as they rise—interest rates and labor costs are prime illustrations. Thus, their rapid increase would tend to depress Mr. Moore's ratio and signal economic constraints ahead for many businesses.

An example of the value of knowing which economic

statistics provide useful indications of future business trends—and which do not—occurred in 1975. Someone trying to fathom the likely course of the slumping economy in, say, early June of that year could easily have become bewildered by economic headlines that at first glance seemed wildly contradictory. At the end of May, the government announced that its new index of leading indicators rose by a record amount in April, the latest month for which the index was available. But a few days later another government report showed that companies were scaling back their capital-spending plans sharply. And the next day it was announced that unemployment in May jumped to 9.2 per cent of the labor force, the highest rate in 34 years.

Different economic yardsticks were giving off diametrically opposite signals. Accordingly, it was important to understand which yardsticks to monitor closely and which largely to disregard. Two that most decidedly are not indicative of the future economic course, especially in a time of deep recession, are capital-spending plans and the unemployment rate. Both tend to lag the general economic trend at such times. They often continue to worsen after business generally has started to improve.

Anyone attempting to stay abreast of the economic outlook in June, 1975, would have been wise to devote relatively little attention to those indicators and instead to keep an eye on the index of leading indicators. It rose a record 4.2 per cent in April. Its April level—95.3, on a base of 1967 = 100—was up from 91.5 in March and 90.6 in February. The February level marked the low point in a decline that began all the way back in July, 1973, four months before the recession set in.

Anyone at all familiar with the record of the composite index would have found the rise since February most en-

couraging. Rarely had the index, after sinking to a recession low point, risen for two months and then started to
decline again. The yardstick to have been watching was
the leading-indicator index. The message that it flashed
loud and clear in June, 1975, was that the long recession
was about over and that a period of renewed economic
expansion seemed at hand.

It is important to point out, however, that the magnitude of the record April rise in the composite index
should not have been taken necessarily as evidence that a
particularly strong, long-lasting economic upturn was
ahead. The 4.2 per cent rise in the composite index broke
a record monthly increase of 3 per cent set in June,
1958—near the start of one of the shortest business expansions ever. There is broad agreement that, while leading indicators show the likely direction of the economy,
they are not especially helpful in determining how sharp
or enduring any change of course may turn out to be.
That question can only be answered as a recovery pro-
gresses, by a careful scrutiny of major components of the
economy.

"There's simply no telling how bad a recession is going
to be until you're into it," says Geoffrey Moore. The vigor
of an expansionary phase in the business cycle is, by the
same token, difficult to predetermine.

The usefulness of the various economic indicators is
also limited by the fact that they generally do not provide
nearly as long a signal before recovery periods as before
recessions. As noted, the composite index of leading indicators, on the average, has signaled recoveries by only
four months, less than half the length of the warning
given prior to recessions. A few leading indicators, to be
sure, have usually given much longer notice of recovery
periods. Among these are the money supply, expressed

as M-1 in constant dollars, and the series showing building permits for private housing units. Each indicator, on the average, has turned up eight months before a rise in overall business. Many leading indicators, in contrast, normally begin to climb only a month or two before the economy turns up. These include, among others, the average workweek, new orders for consumer goods, the layoff rate, new business formations, and new orders for plants and machinery.

*     *     *

Despite these and other shortcomings, the various indicators do provide a remarkably convenient and uncomplicated means by which interested laymen, along with degree-laden economists, may intelligently keep abreast of—indeed, keep ahead of—the movement of the economy. You do not need to be an economist and you do not need to know how to operate a computer.

As the National Bureau's Mr. Moore has said, "judgment will still have to be used in assessing the behavior of the indicators." Virtually all of these are available in *Business Conditions Digest,* a most valuable publication that may be obtained by writing for a yearly subscription to the Superintendent of Documents, U.S. Government Printing Office, Washington, D.C. 20402.

As we will see in the next chapter, there are far more expensive ways to try to keep abreast of the economic outlook. None, we submit, is better than simply doing it yourself, with the help of a daily newspaper, such as *The Wall Street Journal* or, if you live in the New York area, *The New York Times*—plus the monthly issues of *BCD.* The effort requires remarkably little of your time. You may also avoid, in the process, a lot of very bad forecasts.

To rely on economic indicators, in the final analysis, is to rely on common sense. Geoffrey Moore, writing in the

January, 1975, issue of *Scientific American,* discussed, among other things, the reason that such statistical series as housing starts, new orders for machinery, and contracts for new construction projects all usually show an increase several months before the economy in general picks up. "It takes time to build a house or a factory or a turbine," he observed. "The actual production or completion or shipping usually lags behind the orders and contracts." It is that "actual production," of course, that determines the overall level of business activity in the country—in effect, the particular phase of the cycle that business happens to be in. As we have seen, we can be reasonably sure that business will be always in one phase or the other, expanding or contracting.

Chapter 7

# FORECASTS

It is possible, we have observed, to gain valuable insights into the likely future behavior of the economy by simply keeping track of various economic indicators. Moreover, one need not be a degree-laden economist to follow these indicators and, using them, to ascertain the probable direction of the business cycle.

We have seen, in effect, that you can do it yourself. The necessary statistical information is readily available. And it can be assessed and used to form sound conclusions—without the need of expertise.

The layman who seeks perspective on the economy and its likely course should also make an effort, however, to peruse at least a few of the economic forecasts that regularly emanate from experts. For there assuredly is no shortage of highly trained economists who make a business—frequently high priced and highly profitable—of monitoring every statistical series mentioned in this book, and many more besides. They apply their expertise to digest all the data and then come up with periodic forecasts of how the economic trend is likely to develop. The forecasts may range over developments in coming months or years or even decades. Mostly, however, forecasters limit their predictions to periods not beyond 12 months.

164

Within that span, they generally provide detailed estimates regarding such matters as the likely level of the GNP and the real GNP, the likely rate of unemployment, probable changes in the consumer price index, and so on. One area that economists often eschew in their forecasts is the stock market. As we have noted, share-price indexes can behave in the short run in a highly volatile fashion, and most economists are understandably wary about trying to predict such volatile movements in any precise detail.

## Lots of Prophets

The layman who wishes to keep abreast of expert views on the economic future should have no difficulty. The daily newspapers contain forecasts. Major banks and securities firms employ analysts who produce frequent appraisals of the business outlook. Often, these forecasts are freely available to customers who merely express an interest in obtaining them. Corporations also employ forecasters whose main job is to advise top executives about general business prospects. Often this advice is kept within the corporation. But some major concerns do publish their forecasts. General Electric, Prudential Life, and RCA are examples.

A notable exception is IBM, the computer giant, whose chief economist, David Grove, is among the more reticent forecasters in the nation.

Among major banks, Chase Manhattan, Manufacturers Hanover, and First National City, all in New York, and Bank of America in San Francisco turn out a variety of material on a regular basis that appraises the economic climate. First National City, particularly, prides itself on the excellence of its economics department and the profusion of material, much of it readily available to the public, that the department turns out each month. The bank's chief economist, Leif H. Olsen, happens to be a former financial journalist, with experience at both *The Wall Street Journal* and *The New York Times*. This background, I suspect, has a lot to do with the easy readability of First National City's economic appraisals.

Most prominent business forecasters make at least some of their reports freely available to major newspapers, if not to the public in general. But only a fraction of this material actually finds its way into the financial pages. Many newspapers devote only limited space to any sort of economic news. Their business coverage often consists largely of reporting the latest stock and bond prices. Some forecasts do find their way, fortunately, into such newspapers as *The Wall Street Journal, The New York Times, The Washington Post,* and *The Los Angeles Times.* But even in these newspapers, what appears is usually a minuscule fraction of what is received in newsrooms around the country. If its editors so chose, *The Wall Street Journal,* my employer, could print nothing but economic predictions on all of its pages every day of the week. Wisely, its editors have long exercised considerable discretion in deciding which forecasts should be run in whole or in part each day and which should best be relegated to the wastebasket.

One type of forecast is rarely relegated to *The Wall Street Journal*'s wastebasket. That is the forecast made by a high government official, such as the President, the Chairman of his Council of Economic Advisers, the Treasury Secretary or the Chairman of the Federal Reserve Board. The reasoning among most editors—quite logically—is that such individuals are in positions where they can actually influence future economic activity, and this

FORECASTS 167

ability lends considerable weight to their forecasts. If the Chairman of the Federal Reserve Board says that he believes the economy is about to move from a recessionary phase to a period of expansion, the prediction is deemed highly significant, because the Fed Chairman actually has the power to spur economic growth through adopting a more expansionary monetary policy. He also may be privy to information about the economy not yet generally available.

Suffice it to say that the interested layman who wishes to expand his perspective on the business outlook—gained, one would hope, through a careful observation of the appropriate economic indicators—may do so by keeping a tab on the various forecasts reported in major newspapers. He may further broaden his perspective by obtaining, often at no charge, forecasts made by selected banks, securities concerns, and large corporations.

*    *    *

Different forecasters use different forecasting methods. Some go through a more elaborate version of the process that anyone familiar with the important indicators described in this book can readily perform. Others go far beyond scrutinizing the indicators and set up esoteric mathematical equations—"models" of the overall economy, in effect, constructed with such building blocks as the GNP and the inflation rate.

These equations are fed into computers which, in short order, spew out all sorts of information about the future shape of the economy. These "econometric" forecasts (which reflect the merging of mathematics, statistics and economics) can be especially useful to individual corporations; computers can be set to predict economic developments down to such details as the number of shoes likely to be sold during a six-month period. Such information, while of dubious interest or use to most citizens, would presumably be of considerable concern to a shoe manufacturer.

The differing methods that forecasters use to reach their estimates of the business outlook are noted by the National Bureau's Mr. Moore, who—perhaps wisely—does exceedingly little forecasting himself. "Analysis of economic indicators is one way of assessing" the economic outlook, he says, and "econometric models of the business-cycle process are another."

Which of the many available forecasts should the interested layman follow?

There is, unfortunately, no short, simple answer. A list of forecasters with considerable reputations might include, among others, James J. O'Leary of U.S. Trust Co., A. Gilbert Heebner of Philadelphia National Bank, Robert Ortner of Bank of New York, Beryl W. Sprinkel of Harris Trust in Chicago, Morris Cohen of Schroder Naess & Thomas in New York, Charles Reeder of Du Pont Co., A. Gary Shilling of White, Weld & Co. in New York, and Frank Murphy of General Electric.

To this list might be added several of the relatively new firms that specialize in detailed econometric forecasting for business customers. Among these are Data Resources of Lexington, Mass., run by the same Otto Eckstein who once took me to task over that recession article, Chase Econometrics of Philadelphia, headed by a highly energetic and outspoken young economist named Michael K. Evans, and the Wharton School's Economic Forecasting Unit, run by Lawrence Klein, an economics professor at the University of Pennsylvania's prestigious business school.

All of these individuals and organizations, whether they merely analyze indicators or rely on complex computer techniques, make their predictions freely available to the major newspapers and, partly as a result, receive wide attention. There is no question that their views on the economic future are well worth monitoring.

However, I should emphasize that there is no substitute for keeping abreast of the important statistics yourself, and trying to understand how the business cycle may develop. For it is a fact that many of the business prophets are occasionally more than slightly inaccurate in their forecasts. Moreover, like the rest of us, forecasters for various reasons do not always proclaim in public what they may be telling their employers in private. This is all the more reason that you should, basically, try to do it yourself, as far as assessing the economic outlook is concerned.

## Shortcomings

Various studies have been conducted in recent years to try to determine precisely how accurate business forecasters have been. The studies show a considerably less than perfect record. Beware of the forecaster who does not employ an ample amount of modesty and caution in predicting the economic course. The proper approach should be along the line used by Gilbert Heebner of Philadelphia National Bank. Making a "midyear outlook" report in June, 1975, the economist began: "Economists should approach the current midyear forecast with an extra measure of humility. For it was only a year ago that the profession erred so badly in failing to predict the sharp drop that began last fall." Mr. Heebner maintained that "it is always a healthy exercise for an economist to ask: If his or her forecast should err—a not-infrequent occurrence—in which direction is it likely to err, and why?"

A survey conducted by *Business Week* in December, 1973, makes clear how badly highly trained forecasters can occasionally err. The magazine published the estimates of 32 prominent forecasters for the economy in 1974. Among other details, the survey showed each one's forecast for the real GNP and for price changes during 1974. Only one of the 32—and he deserves to be named: A. Gary Shilling of White, Weld—forecast a decline in the real GNP during 1974. Mr. Shilling predicted a 1.5 per cent drop in that coincident indicator; in fact, it fell nearly twice that much during the year.

Many of the 31 other forecasters predicted substantial increases in the real GNP.

Even more lamentable was the group's record on the price front. In 1974, prices actually rose more than 10 per cent, on the average. But none of the 32 forecasters anticipated double-digit inflation. The highest rate of price increase forecast by anyone was 7.5 per cent. One unfortunate fellow, a professor of economics at Princeton University who relies heavily on econometric techniques, forecast a price climb of only 4.7 per cent in 1974. The same forecaster also predicted that the real GNP would rise a healthy 3.5 per cent in the year.

To be fair, 1974 was a particularly difficult year for forecasters to envisage. As noted in the previous chapter, inflation badly distorted the movement of leading indicators denominated in dollars.

Over longer intervals, various studies show that the track records of most forecasters are reasonably respectable. In late 1974, the Boston Federal Reserve Bank studied the records of seven prominent forecasting organizations over a four-year period. The Boston Fed found that "despite unusually large forecasting errors recently, the best forecasters have been able to anticipate the growth of

GNP and real GNP with an average absolute error of 1 per cent."

In the January, 1975, issue of a business review published by Morgan Guaranty Trust, Geoffrey Moore reviewed the forecasting records of government economists as well as those of many analysts employed by private businesses. He concluded that "the two groups seem to use the same crystal ball." It is clear, he stated, that "economists can point to a creditable performance over the years in forecasting output." However, he added, "in forecasting prices, clearly there is much room for improvement."

The National Bureau analyst also noted that the forecasters in both the groups have tended over the years "to err in their predictions on the side of optimism—both tend to overestimate output and to underestimate the probable increase in the price level." Certainly, undue optimism prevailed in that *Business Week* survey in December, 1973.

\* \* \*

This tendency toward overoptimism is important to bear in mind when one peruses forecasts. One need not look far to understand why the tendency exists. An anecdote involving a major securities concern suggests one explanation. It involves the aforementioned Gary Shilling.

I first came to know Mr. Shilling back in the late 1960s, when he was chief economist—at the astoundingly young age of 29—for the nation's largest and, in the view of many, most prestigious Wall Street securities firm, Merrill Lynch, Pierce, Fenner and Smith. John Allan, a financial reporter on *The New York Times* and a former colleague at *The Wall Street Journal,* had mentioned Mr. Shilling to me as a man who correctly predicted, almost to the day, a generally unexpected devaluation of the British pound.

This was no mean achievement back in the years when key currency exchange rates were fixed in relation to one another, and therefore unlikely to change from one week to the next, as often happens now.

Appropriately impressed, I made it a point to get in touch with this bright young analyst. By 1969 I had become a staunch admirer of his forecasting abilities. Little did I imagine that this admiration would eventually place Mr. Shilling in a most uncomfortable situation at Merrill Lynch.

The trouble began on a bright December morning, a day or two before Christmas, 1969. The Merrill Lynch economist called to wish me a merry Christmas and also to express his not-so-merry doubts about the country's economic prospects. He told me, among other things, that he fully anticipated—and I use his adjective—a "major" recession just ahead. This was a considerably more gloomy position than that held by most economic forecasters at the time. The consensus was that no recession impended. Even relatively pessimistic members of the forecasting fraternity felt any slowdown that might occur surely would constitute only a mild interruption in the ongoing business expansion. At least that is what was generally stated publicly.

Mr. Shilling, of course, turned out to be eminently correct. A major recession, as we noted earlier, did indeed begin in late 1969, and it persisted and deepened for about a year. The Merrill Lynch economist's prescient warning appeared under my byline on December 26, 1969. The headline read: "Merrill Lynch Chief Economist Sees Business Headed into Major Recession."

Donald T. Regan, who ran Merrill Lynch at that time, as he still does, was highly upset to find his chief economist predicting publicly a major recession—and, no shrinking violet, he let Mr. Shilling know about it in blunt terms. The economist recalls, among other things, that his bonus—in those days, an important part of yearly compensation at many Wall Street firms—was reduced sharply a short time after the recession forecast was published. In the ensuing weeks, as the recession materialized, I noticed that Mr. Shilling's forecasts became rarer and rarer and, when they did sporadically surface, seemed blander and more cautious. He found himself involved in a variety of in-house projects, including special assignments for Mr. Regan that allowed him little time for economic forecasting. Eventually, he found himself no longer the firm's chief economist, but merely one of several economists assigned not to the parent company but to a recently acquired investment-advisory subsidiary, Lionel D. Edie & Co. Soon thereafter, Mr. Shilling quit his Merrill Lynch employment. He is now chief economist at White, Weld, a Wall Street securities firm that competes for business with Merrill Lynch. (In fairness, it should be noted that a Merrill Lynch spokesman says it was not the substance of the Shilling forecast but the manner in which it was released—prematurely to the press—that "irked everyone." As for the reduced bonus, the spokesman says Merrill Lynch suffered a sharp decline in its earnings that year.)

Still, the lesson for anyone who follows the forecasts of economists employed by private businesses seems plain enough. Be aware that such economists can easily antagonize their bosses if they sound too pessimistic about the business outlook—at least in public. Ridiculous as it may seem, many businessmen apparently believe that gloomy forecasts can actually create a gloomy economy. By the same token, there are many executives who seem to think that by producing optimistic forecasts, economists can somehow raise the general level of business activity.

If there is any truth at all in such ideas, the amount must be minuscule. In any event, it is a wise procedure to bear in mind the pressures that may force some economists, who may actually be pessimistic about business prospects, to remain silent—or, much worse, to sound more optimistic in public than they feel in private.

\*   \*   \*

The same tendency toward overoptimism, not surprisingly, prevails among forecasters employed by the administration that happens to be in power in Washington. With notable—and noble—exceptions, such officials invariably try to be more sanguine than economic facts may justify. Typical of this habit were the repeated predictions of Herbert Stein, President Nixon's chief economic adviser in the early 1970s, that inflation would soon begin to abate. Again and again, the Nixon economist told the electorate what it presumably enjoyed hearing—that inflation would soon ease. And again and again he turned out to be wrong. Rather than abating, inflation intensified painfully during Mr. Stein's tenure in Washington.

After departing Washington, the economist took up duties as an occasional columnist for *The Wall Street Journal*. Writing as a private citizen, he seems far more concerned about the possibility of worsening inflation than he appeared to be during his speech-making days at the White House, when warnings of a worsening price spiral were fully warranted but not forthcoming.

There are, in addition, occasional instances where a forecast may be unduly pessimistic because of political pressures on the forecaster. I recall such a situation in early 1971, when the economy was just beginning to pull out of the 1969–70 recession. A prominent economics

professor, who had served as an adviser to President
Johnson and was still closely tied to the Democratic party,
was publicly lambasting the Nixon administration for
what the professor claimed were woefully inadequate policies that would surely perpetuate the recession. If taken
seriously, these forecasts would have chilled any optimism
about business prospects that a layman might have acquired, say, by simply following the climb of various leading indicators at that time.

Quite by chance, I discovered that the professor also
served as a consultant to a New York-based brokerage
house, one of whose executives is an old friend. My
stockbroker friend, I was aware, was reasonably—and, as
things turned out, rightly—optimistic about the economic
outlook. I asked him how this optimism squared with the
obvious gloom expressed by the firm's consultant. My
friend's reply: "We know that in his public statements he
has been sharply critical of Nixon's economic performance, charging that the President isn't doing nearly
enough to get the economy out of the recession. However, his private advice to us, for which we pay him a considerable retainer, has sounded like this—the Nixon team
has done a good job of getting inflation under control
without letting the recession get too deep, the business
outlook is very good, with a prolonged period of economic expansion in prospect, and you should therefore
get your clients invested in sound stocks."

A similar episode of more recent vintage involves Senator Hubert Humphrey, in his highly visible role as chairman of the Joint Economic Committee of Congress. In
mid-1975, when the leading indicators unmistakably
pointed upward toward a recovery period, Senator
Humphrey, in his committee role, issued a particularly
gloomy appraisal of the outlook. The appraisal came on

the heels of a Labor Department report that the nation's jobless rate had jumped to 9.2 per cent. He deplored the unemployment rise as a harbinger of still worse economic times ahead. Among other things, he gloomily forecast that "there is no employment rise in sight."

In fact, a recovery in employment was already under way. The same report that showed a rise in the unemployment rate to 9.2 per cent also disclosed, in the fine print, a 316,000 jump in employment, on top of a 237,000 employment increase the month before. The Humphrey statement made no mention of this rise in employment. As we saw earlier, employment changes can tell more about general economic conditions than changes in the jobless rate.

The message is clear. Anyone attempting to keep abreast of the economic outlook through observing published forecasts should do so gingerly. If the forecaster, like Senator Humphrey, happens to be a political opponent of the administration in the White House, be wary of excessive pessimism. If the forecaster, like Herbert Stein, is employed by the White House, look out for too much optimism. And if the forecaster works for a profit-making organization whose boss may believe—rightly or wrongly—that gloomy forecasts can hurt business, again be wary of overoptimism.

## Credentials

Before leaving the matter of forecasting, a few words are in order about credentials. All through this chapter, I have stressed that most widely-followed forecasters are "degree-laden" and "highly trained." A primary message of this book, of course, is to emphasize precisely that you do not need to be "degree-laden" or "highly trained" to appraise the economic scene intelligently. It is true that most successful forecasters are indeed laden with degrees in economics. But one should bear in mind that there are major exceptions. This can be readily illustrated by recalling predictions made in 1973 by two widely followed but remarkably disparate forecasters.

The forecasting game, like many other endeavors, attracts wildly diverse players. The disparate forecasters that I have in mind are Robert H. Parks, serving in 1973 as chief economist of Blyth Eastman Dillon & Co., a large, well-known New York securities concern, and Harry D. Schultz, the publisher of an economic newsletter with several thousand loyal subscribers. The credentials of the two forecasters are strikingly dissimilar.

Bob Parks' credentials are, to say the least, impressive. The "doctor" that he uses before his name is well earned. His credentials include a doctorate and a master's degree from the University of Pennsylvania, a bachelor's degree from Swarthmore, and professorships at two universities.

Not so with Harry Schultz. He once told a *Wall Street Journal* reporter—who accepted it—that the "doctor" he uses before his name reflects a doctorate he received from St. Lawrence University in New York State. But his name is utterly unknown to officials at St. Lawrence. "We find no indication that one Mr. Harry Schultz ever attended St. Lawrence University at any time or that he ever received an honorary degree from this university," declares an official of the Canton, N.Y., institution. It does appear that Harry Schultz did spend a couple of years at City College of Los Angeles, where he majored not in economics or finance, but journalism.

So, the question arises: Which man's view of the economic future would you tend to heed—that of Dr. Parks or that of "Dr." Schultz?

In mid-1973, if you had been listening to Bob Parks over the past year or so, you would probably have kept much of your money invested in the U.S. stock market— and taken your lumps along with most investors. As we saw earlier in that *Business Week* survey, Bob Parks assuredly was not alone among respected analysts in 1973 in his optimism about general business prospects.

"Dr." Schultz, on the other hand, was dispensing some uncannily prescient advice to his subscribers in 1973. His letters dripped in gloom about the economic outlook. One suggested "portfolio" of his, consisting wholly of South African gold-mining shares, had appreciated more than 200 per cent since the beginning of 1972. Another, made up largely of securities from such countries as France and Switzerland, but without a single share of U.S. stock, had climbed about 20 per cent just since the start of 1973, a period in which prices of most U.S. stocks dropped sharply.

Looking ahead in mid-1973, with much rough economic weather to come, Bob Parks remained relatively optimistic. One Parks appraisal of economic prospects, for example, expressed the belief that "this expansion [of economic activity] will turn out to be one of the longest in U.S. history." He was utterly wrong, of course; the expansion ended in November of that very year. He also opined that President Nixon's actions on the price front [to initiate a series of price-control moves in August, 1971] "visibly and believably" strengthened the country's "attack on inflation." In fact, inflation worsened severely in the year or so after the Parks forecast.

"Dr." Harry Schultz, in mid-1973, saw the outlook differently. One report, almost comical in the degree of its pessimism, began: "Civilization, as we know it, is crumbling." Regarding the U.S. stock market, he advised "short positions." He commented that "even in 1930 there were rallies." Regarding his favorite metal, gold—a traditional haven for economic pessimists—he appeared confident that its price would be heading upward in the months to come—and it most certainly did rise.

The gloom expressed by Harry Schultz in 1973 may have been more than a little excessive; publishers of economic newsletters often tend to be overly pessimistic, apparently in the belief that this tactic attracts more subscribers. In any case, that Harry Schultz was largely correct about the economic future in 1973 provides a valuable lesson for anyone who may be tempted to pick forecasters solely on the basis of how many economic degrees they possess or how well known their firms may be.

\*     \*     \*

Altogether, it is clear that to follow economic forecasts blindly is a risky undertaking. Forecasters with impressive credentials can be entirely wrong about the outlook, while forecasters with seemingly unimpressive credentials—or credentials that turn out to be false—can prove to be correct.

A few successful economists are so wary about trying to predict the precise movement of the business cycle that they simply refuse to issue detailed forecasts at all.

One such analyst is Edward C. Harwood, founder of an economic research concern in Great Barrington, Mass. In elaborating on his position, the economist explains that "we do not join in the annual forecasting derby that is so popular among economists, pseudo-economists, and business analysts near the beginning of each new year. . . . Neither we nor anyone else that we know of has developed a scientific basis for predicting with a useful degree of accuracy the levels that gross national product, the industrial production index, stock market averages or other measures of economic activity will reach six months or a year in the future. Of course, computers will provide such projections with remarkable speed, but the final printout of a computer is no more accurate in foreseeing the future than are the assumptions and guesses of the individuals who develop the input program. Also, because we have not discovered any reliable method for predicting these short-term fluctuations in the various aspects of economic activity, we do not attempt to give trading advice to investors or recommend frequent changes in an investment portfolio in the hope of making quick profits."

Mr. Harwood contents himself by assuming that inflation, despite occasional periods of abatement, will continue to worsen and erode the dollar's buying power. He believes that the prudent investor should concentrate on ways to limit this erosion, rather than worry about whether the business cycle happens to be in an up-phase or a down-phase.

Such a strategy, if nothing else, protects Mr. Harwood from the embarrassment, suffered in 1973 by Bob Parks, of producing woefully wrong forecasts. It also keeps him comfortably aloof from the nasty sort of backbiting that unhappily pervades the forecasting game. I once obtained a front-row view of this widespread practice among forecasters. I had mentioned in a *Wall Street Journal* column in mid-1974 that Gary Shilling anticipated an unemployment rate of 8 per cent or more in coming months. At the time, with actual unemployment just above 5 per cent of the labor force, it was a rather daring forecast for anyone to make, even an economist with Mr. Shilling's good track record.

Soon after the column appeared, I received an angry letter from Mike Evans of Chase Econometrics. Mr.

Evans, whom I barely knew, attacked at length Mr. Shilling's competence as a forecaster. Among other charges, the Chase Econometrics president declared that "I view his 8 per cent unemployment rate forecast as being [much too high] and dead wrong." Less than six months after the Evans letter arrived, the unemployment rate crossed above 8 per cent, and less than a year after the letter, the rate stood at 9.2 per cent.

Perhaps the one thing more embarrassing for a forecaster than issuing a dead-wrong forecast is to be dead wrong in claiming that a colleague's forecast is dead wrong. That is the sort of embarrassment that Mr. Harwood in his Great Barrington office, in the rolling hills of western Massachusetts, runs no danger of suffering.

## Chapter 8

# FOREIGNERS

JOHN DONNE, the 17th-century British poet, once observed that "no man is an island, entire of it self." He went on to caution that one should "never send to know for whom the bell tolls; it tolls for thee."

Thus far, our attention has largely been focused on ways of gauging the approximate level and likely future development of economic activity within the U.S. Had this book been written, say, a quarter-century ago, there would have been little need for this chapter. The U.S. economy, in those bygone days, could have been appraised well enough through simply remaining abreast of appropriate economic gauges designed to measure the health of U.S. business.

The U.S. economy 25 or 30 years ago, in an economic sense, was still a sort of island. It was an island in that its size and strength, in relation to other economies, was so overwhelming that it was largely impervious to economic developments elsewhere. It was an island in another sense—on account of the exceptional monetary arrangements under which international business was transacted. These arrangements, as we will see, were highly advantageous to the U.S. For many years, they served to insulate the country from some of the nastier consequences of its own economic policies.

Now, a very different economic world has emerged, in which no important country can be an economic island. When the bell tolls now, it does so for all the major economies. Nowadays, any attempt to understand the U.S. economy necessitates keeping track of economic developments abroad as well as at home. This can be easily done—though it must be said that no other country maintains the profusion of reasonably reliable economic yardsticks that U.S. analysts have managed to assemble.

In this chapter, we will try to trace the increasing interdependence of the U.S. economy and those elsewhere. We will, further, offer some suggestions on how best to follow the diverse, often puzzling foreign picture.

## No Island

In the third chapter, we briefly discussed the international value of the U.S. dollar as a useful barometer of the health of the American economy. It was noted, among other things, that the dollar's international value—that is, its price in terms of other currencies—nowadays moves up or down largely in response to ever-changing forces of supply and demand. The dollar tends to appreciate in terms of other currencies when demand for it is on the rise. And it tends to decline in terms of other currencies when foreign demand for it lags. In effect, the dollar's international value tends to "float"—to use an expression of economists—in relation to other currencies.

This floating arrangement has existed only since 1971. In earlier years after World War II, the international value of the U.S. dollar did not float. Instead, it was arbitrarily fixed, under international agreement, at a level of $35 per ounce of gold. This so-called fixed-rate system was set up at an international monetary conference held at Bretton Woods, N.H., in 1944. Under the system, U.S. officials were to try to keep the value of the dollar fixed at $35 per ounce of gold, and other major countries were to try to keep the values of their particular currencies fixed in terms of the dollar.

The upshot, at least in theory, was that all currencies were fixed in terms of one another. The U.S., with a huge supply of gold at the end of World War II, stood ready to buy or sell the yellow metal in transactions with other governments at a rate of $35 per ounce. At the same time, other governments stood ready to buy or sell dollars in such a way as to maintain the agreed-upon fixed relationships between their currencies and the dollar. A commercial bank in Country X would, under the fixed-rate system, turn in dollars to Country X's central bank and, in return, receive googols, the Country X currency, at whatever happened to be the fixed rate of exchange between the dollar and the googol.

As things developed, this fixed-rate arrangement served to insulate the U.S. from inflationary pressures that might otherwise have developed within the American economy. Instead, these pressures were transmitted out of the U.S. and developed abroad. Exactly how this transmission occurred can best be illustrated, perhaps, by recalling events in West Germany in 1971, the year in which the Bretton Woods system of fixed rates fell apart.

On May 5 of that year, the Bundesbank, West Germany's central bank, stopped buying dollars for marks and, in effect, let the dollar float downward in relation to the mark. By so doing, the German government abandoned Bretton Woods procedure. In the 48 hours beforehand, West German officials later explained, the Bundesbank had been obliged by Bretton Woods rules to buy more than $2 billion at the fixed dollar-mark rate of exchange, issuing marks for the U.S. currency. They complained bitterly at the time that such forced buying of dollars for marks was exacerbating inflation in their country by causing the German money supply to rise at about twice the desired rate.

The West German experience of May, 1971, illustrates how inflation could be exported under the Bretton Woods arrangement. Dollars poured into Germany far in excess of what German officials deemed healthy for their country's economy. Otmar Emminger, a governor of the Bundesbank, estimated at the time that West Germany's money supply was growing at an annual rate of more than 20 per cent in the spring of 1971, a period when a monetary growth rate of about 10 per cent appeared appropriate.

Under Bretton Woods procedure, West German officials could have asked the U.S. government for gold, at the $35 price, for the unwanted dollars at the Bundesbank—piling up there as Americans continued to spend and invest heavily in West Germany. In practice, however, West Germany—as well as other foreign countries similarly inundated—was hesitant to make such a request because, bluntly, it had become increasingly clear that America's dwindling gold supply could no longer meet the potential demands of dollar-holders abroad.

The inevitable result of this bind was the West German decision, followed by similar ones elsewhere, to stop buying dollars for marks. Later in 1971, in another inevitable move, the U.S. officially abandoned its long-standing pledge to buy or sell gold at the $35 figure.

*      *      *

Now, since the Bretton Woods system has collapsed, currency values float daily in relation to one another, largely in response to the forces of supply and demand. No government is obliged to swallow American dollars at a fixed rate of exchange if dollars pile up there. Now, when the Federal Reserve's monetary policy becomes overly expansionary, much of the resulting inflationary pressure must stay home. Such inflation no longer may be readily exported, as before, to such places as West Germany. Accordingly, excessive dollars now will more quickly generate domestic inflation. Under today's circumstances, the dollar's value in international currency markets would be likelier to drop if Fed policy is overly expansionary. And any such drop would likely intensify inflationary pressures at home, inasmuch as it would make imported goods costlier for Americans and spur demand for U.S.-made products abroad.

The precise inflationary impact of any sharp rise in the U.S. money supply, to be sure, would depend on a variety of imponderables. These range from how cleanly the dollar is allowed to float in relation to other currencies— without interference in international currency markets by central-banking authorities—to how expansionary the policies of other governments happen to be. The international value of the dollar, to illustrate, would presumably hold up better if policies of rapid monetary growth happen to be pursued in other countries. As a result of the change from fixed to floating rates, those who determine U.S. economic policy nowadays must proceed more cautiously than in the Bretton Woods era. They must keep a sharper watch on economic developments abroad—and the same applies for the individual who wishes to keep abreast.

A few words should perhaps be inserted here to point out that considerable disagreement exists among economists over whether a fixed-rate system or a floating-rate arrangement is more inflationary for the world as a whole. Proponents of a fixed-rate system point to the fact that inflation in most countries worsened considerably after the Bretton Woods system collapsed in 1971.

Analysts who favor floating rates contend that much of the world's post-1971 inflation derives from practices in effect during the Bretton Woods years, when the U.S. was pumping all those dollars abroad. In fact, these analysts blame much of the post-1971 inflation precisely on the huge hoard of American dollars that accumulated abroad under the fixed-rate system. Many of these dollars, it is observed, still are on deposit in European banks and elsewhere, under the label of Eurodollars. It is generally agreed that these Eurodollars—exceeding the $200 billion mark—have contributed greatly to inflationary pressure throughout the world in recent years. Advocates of floating exchange rates argue that the pileup of Eurodollars never would have reached such proportions without the fixed-rate system.

Whatever the merits of the opposing viewpoints, the fact is that in today's world of floating rates, the U.S. government cannot pursue inflationary policies with impunity. As economist Milton Friedman once observed, "fixed rates allow inflationary policies to be disguised."

\*     \*     \*

The advent of floating exchange rates is merely one manifestation of the rising economic interdependence of the major economies. This interdependence shows up in other ways as well. U.S. foreign trade figures provide one illustration. In 1960, U.S. exports amounted to only about 5 per cent of the country's gross national product, and U.S. imports constituted an even smaller percentage of the GNP. By 1974, as international commerce continued to expand extra rapidly, U.S. exports alone amounted to about 10 per cent of the GNP, twice the 1960 rate. Clearly, foreign trade has become an important factor in the country's economic picture. Accordingly, a sharp drop in the country's export volume today would unquestionably have a much more severe impact on American jobs and general prosperity than such a drop would have had, say, in 1960. In the same manner, as U.S. imports have risen, so has the importance of the American economy to many businesses and workers abroad.

In a recent period, roughly 25 per cent of cars sold in the U.S. were manufactured abroad. This remarkably high rate leaves little doubt that any severe cutback in U.S. spending for automobiles could have serious economic consequences in auto-producing countries abroad.

Most forecasters expect the role of foreign trade within the U.S. economic picture to continue to expand. Otto Eckstein of Data Resources says that "the health of the world economy will be of increasing importance to the United States" in the years just ahead. He anticipates that U.S. exports will constitute a larger and larger share of the country's expanding GNP. By 1990, the economist estimates, exports will amount to about 16 per cent of the GNP. He forecasts that imports will expand at roughly the same rate as exports. In absolute terms, however, exports are expected to exceed imports by a considerable margin, so that the country will have what economists call a trade surplus. As we observed in the third chapter, such surpluses normally suggest that the overall economy is in relatively sound shape.

Other statistics underline the rising economic importance of international investment flows, as well as international trade, to the U.S. An estimated 21 per cent of private investments made in the U.S. in 1973, for example, were made by foreigners. That compares with a figure of only 7 per cent ten years earlier, in 1963, and less than 4 per cent fifteen years earlier, in 1958. A similar rise in foreign investing in various government-type securities, such as Treasury bills, is also apparent from other statistics.

The considerable role that foreign investors now occupy on the U.S. economic stage means, among other things, that business decisions affecting American jobs and prosperity more often are being taken by foreigners. It is far likelier today that a decision, say, to build a new American automobile plant may depend, at least in part, on economic and political conditions in West Germany or Japan or France or Sweden.

The major illustration of this interdependence spreading beyond just the highly industrialized economies occurred in 1973. That was when the Middle Eastern oil-producing countries demanded—with resounding success—sharply higher prices for their oil. The move made clear the extent to which key economies, including the exceedingly powerful U.S. economy, have become linked to business and political decisions made far from New York or London or Frankfurt or Paris or Tokyo.

The decision to increase petroleum prices so sharply—and even for a while to withhold petroleum shipments—caused unimagined economic repercussions in the U.S. and elsewhere. There were, of course, the long lines at gasoline stations. Families in New York saw their electricity bills soar. Executives in Detroit saw sales of their high-powered, gas-guzzling cars plunge. As noted earlier, it can be argued convincingly that the recent deep recession which started in November, 1973, set in much sooner than might otherwise have been the case. Many economists believe that, without the oil squeeze, the 1970–73 economic expansion would have kept going until at least mid-1974.

Impressed by the success of the oil-producing countries in raising petroleum prices, countries producing a wide range of other important industrial raw materials—for instance bauxite, used in making aluminum—will likely be driving harder and harder bargains in their trade negotiations with such commodity-consuming industrial powers as the U.S. These other raw-materials producers may not enjoy the same high degree of success as the oil producers. Few materials are as vital to the industrial countries as oil. However, to the extent that they are successful at all, this will surely affect economic developments in the U.S. and other highly developed nations.

The other side of the coin is that the materials-producing lands themselves are bound to become more important customers for manufactured goods and technological expertise supplied by such countries as the U.S. This is because their wealth will rise along with the rising revenues that their raw materials bring in from the U.S. and elsewhere. The inflow of money will tend to spur spending in these areas, which remain relatively undeveloped in economic terms.

Not surprisingly, U.S. exports to the oil-rich countries of the Middle East already are sharply on the rise. Such increases ultimately should serve to bind still more closely the economies of different nations.

A high degree of economic intertwining is already evident in the fact that the business cycles of the major economies appear to be closely in phase with one another. This has not always been the case.

In the years fairly soon after World War II, in contrast to nowadays, the economies of most countries moved in the same direction at the same time relatively rarely.

America's industrial output index slumped in 1960, for example, and yet industrial output in many major West European countries climbed briskly during that period. More recently, economic activity declined in France in 1968, in Italy in 1969, and in the United Kingdom in 1972—without concurrent economic declines in such other key areas as the U.S. or Japan.

Such disparity, however, has been diminishing in recent years. Indeed, the recent 1973–75 recession appears to have set in at approximately the same time in most industrial lands. Not all the countries entered recessions precisely in November, 1973, the month designated by the National Bureau as the start of the slump in the U.S. But various statistics do indicate that business activity outside the U.S. generally began to contract within a few months, on one side or the other, of the November date. Among countries whose economies slumped around this time were Canada, France, West Germany, Italy and Japan. Together, they account for a considerable portion of worldwide business activity.

This remarkably uniform behavior, in the view of many analysts, reflects mainly the aforementioned growth of international trade and investment, and the consequent intertwining of different economies. Exports, for instance, play an even larger economic role in most countries nowadays than in the U.S. A prime example is West Germany, where export sales rose in a recent 10-year period from 21 per cent of the West German gross national product to 30 per cent.

Looking ahead, the consensus view is that the interdependence of the major economies will continue and grow, and that this interdependence will gradually extend as well to most less-developed economies. Increasing uniformity of world-wide economic developments is forecast by Data Resources. Mr. Eckstein's organization has estimated that the real GNP in the U.S., West Germany, France, Canada, Japan, and Britain will all rise in 1977, and the predicted increases are within a remarkably narrow range. At the high end is Canada, with a projected rise in its real GNP of about 6 per cent. At the bottom end is Britain, with a projected increase of 3 per cent. Four of the six countries are bracketed within less than a percentage point of each other.

Such projections emphasize the importance of trying to keep abreast of economic trends beyond the boundaries of the U.S. To non-economists, that may seem a forbidding endeavor. However, it is not nearly as difficult as one may imagine. Much of the useful information is readily available. In addition, governments and private analysts in many countries are striving to improve the quality and expand the quantity of economic data.

**Watching the World**

We have observed the growing economic interdependence of the major industrial countries. We have seen that good times in the U.S. or West Germany or Japan are likelier nowadays to coincide with good times elsewhere. And, unfortunately, the same thing can be said about bad times. It is not surprising, in view of this interdependence, that a major effort is under way to assemble data that bears on the economic outlook in foreign areas, as well as in the U.S.

Students of the U.S. economy, we have seen, have long had available statistics that indicate in abundant detail the health and likely course of American business. One collection of such data is, as noted earlier, *Business Conditions Digest,* the Commerce Department's monthly publication.

The publication also contains important international statistics—industrial production, consumer price reports, and stock-market movements for more than a half dozen major countries abroad. These statistics provide a simple, fast way for the interested layman to keep up to date on key foreign trends. However, absent from *Business Conditions Digest* is a variety of data that might clearly suggest, for example, whether economic activity in West Germany is likely to accelerate or slow.

One effort to fill this void has been undertaken by the National Bureau of Economic Research. National Bureau economists, directed by Geoffrey Moore, hope that their work will lead to the regular publication of a new monthly report that would do on an international scale what *Business Conditions Digest* has done so well for so long on the American scene. Ideally, National Bureau analysts would like to see such a report published by a prestigious international organization, such as the International Monetary Fund, based in Washington, or the Organization for Economic Cooperation and Development, based in Paris. National Bureau economists have recently discussed the matter with IMF and OECD officials. Conferences have been held in Washington, Paris, Geneva, and Stockholm.

An interesting footnote is that some Communist nations, including East Germany and Russia, have expressed an interest in participating in the statistical effort. Officially, such countries claim not to have the sort of cyclical economic growth that characterizes other nations. In practice, however, it is generally felt that they, too, experience fluctuating business activity; as we have seen, government planners can err as readily as private ones.

The National Bureau has produced a progress report on its work toward establishing international leading indicators. The report, written by Mr. Moore and his colleague, Philip A. Klein, states that "personal interviews have been held with more than 80 individuals" from more than a dozen countries. The report claims that "the notion of reliable leading, coincident and lagging indicators can be shown to apply in many countries outside the United States, where it was developed." The report contains a prototype showing how such a publication might appear. The prototype issue—which has been revised to include many actual statistics—covers 13 foreign countries: Australia, Austria, Belgium, Canada, Denmark, France, West Germany, Ireland, Italy, Japan, the Netherlands, Sweden, and the United Kingdom. Also included is a U.S. section, containing a list of 26 key leading, coincident, and lagging indicators.

The section on Japan, for example, lists 15 leading indicators of that country's economic activity, nine coincident indicators, and six lagging indicators. That is more indicators than even the U.S. section provides. Not found in the U.S. section but given for Japan, for instance, is a ratio of operating profits of industrial companies to their sales. At the same time, some indicators that don't show up for Japan are used for the U.S.—such as a lagging indicator recording the U.S. unemployment rate for persons without jobs at least 15 weeks.

National Bureau economists caution that some indicators tend to behave differently in different countries. In Japan, they note, housing starts, a leading indicator in the U.S., show virtually no cyclical movement. An important feature of the prototype issue is the inclusion of a variety of data involving international commerce. The issue includes not only the trade balance, plus exports and imports, of each country but, with an eye to the future, export and import orders. The National Bureau's progress report notes that the U.S. "is relatively less dependent upon trade than is the case with most other countries."

This effort to set up a regular publication of international economic data is by no means unique. Other efforts are under way. The St. Louis Federal Reserve Bank, for example, brings out a quarterly publication that provides statistical information on about nine foreign countries, as well as the U.S. Covered are trends in international trade, production, employment, prices and, most importantly, the money supply. The quarterly publication may be obtained by writing to the St. Louis Fed's research department at Post Office Box 442, St. Louis, Mo. 63166.

Another noteworthy project is the attempt by economists at the University of Pennsylvania's Wharton School to construct a computer-based model of international economic activity. The econometric model, appropriately enough, has been christened Project Link.

The Commerce Department has launched a quarterly publication titled *International Economic Indicators and Competitive Trends.* It does not contain the sort of leading indicators that economists at the National Bureau would like to see developed on an international basis. But it does have much useful data for France, West Germany, Italy, the Netherlands, Britain, Japan, and Canada, as well as the U.S. The coverage includes the real GNP, industrial production, capacity utilization rates, consumer saving rates, export and import figures, various price indexes, balance-of-payments data, and money-supply trends. An annual subscription to the new publication may be obtained through the Superintendent of Documents at the U.S. Government Printing Office, Washington, D.C. 20402, or through any district office of the Commerce Department.

Still another source of important foreign statistics is a

monthly publication of the International Monetary Fund. Called *International Financial Statistics,* it offers a vast range of data covering the organization's more than 100 member nations. The particular advantage of this publication over, say, the Commerce Department's *International Economic Indicators and Competitive Trends* is that it also contains economic information, in varying detail, about so-called less-developed countries. It shows, for instance, that Mauritania's trade balance was in the red to the tune of about one billion *ouguiyas*—the Mauritanian currency—during the third quarter of 1972. Such economic details are hardly of widespread interest to most Americans. But they do illustrate the scope of the IMF publication. It may be obtained from the IMF, Washington, D.C. 20431.

Other international organizations that issue useful economic statistics on a regular basis include the Paris-based Organization for Economic Cooperation and Development and the Brussels-based European Common Market. The only major European country that provides an assortment of leading indicators on a regular basis is the United Kingdom. Britain's Central Statistical Office began in 1975 issuing leading indicators in a publication called *Economic Trends* that is similar to *Business Conditions Digest.* In Asia, the Japanese government also provides such data on a regular basis.

Unfortunately, the United Nations is of little use in this regard. It does issue an array of economic statistics for its many members. However, UN economic statistics generally emerge so long after the fact that they are of limited use to anyone trying to keep a tab on unfolding economic developments at home or abroad.

Various private organizations also regularly provide helpful information that bears on international economic developments. Data Resources, among its many services, periodically issues a *European Review* that contains forecasts and statistical data for the economies of West Germany, France, Britain, Italy, Belgium, the Netherlands, Denmark, and Ireland. A recent review, 143 pages long, included, along with many statistics, discussions by economists of such matters as the impact of higher oil prices and world-wide economic difficulties posed by economic troubles affecting less-developed nations.

Other private outfits that often issue worthwhile appraisals of the international economic scene include, among others, New York's First National City Bank, Lionel D. Edie & Co., Morgan Guaranty Trust, Lombard Odier in Geneva, the New York-based National Foreign Trade Council and, also in New York, Chase Manhattan Bank.

Altogether, the amount of material on international economic matters that is available from governmental and private sources can easily overwhelm anyone who merely may wish to be reasonably well informed about developments. It is unfortunate that no single source, such as *Business Conditions Digest,* exists in the international area. This failing will be remedied in part if the efforts of Mr. Moore and other economists to construct an international counterpart to *BCD* materialize.

*       *       *

Even then, however, the quality of much of the information will likely be less reliable than that of most U.S. data. And we have observed that even U.S. statistics are less than perfect.

The sort of problems encountered in dealing with foreign statistics can be seen by thumbing through the Commerce Department's *International Economic Indicators and Competitive Trends.* In a recent issue, there were no employment figures for France, no unemployment rate for Italy, and no savings statistics for the Netherlands. Money-supply figures for some countries were adjusted for seasonal fluctuations that occur at specified times each year. But figures for other countries were not seasonally adjusted. Moreover, the ways in which each country totaled its money supply varied. The unemployment data contained in the publication also reflected differing methods of computation.

Still, such statistics do give an idea of important trends that may be under way abroad. The Commerce Department effort is certainly a move in the right direction. There is little that U.S. officials can do to improve the compilation of statistics, say, in Italy. Many foreign countries, in addition, have suffered far worse inflation than the U.S. Inflation, we have seen, can distort economic indicators to a point where they may mislead rather than lead.

Trying to keep abreast of economic developments in the less-developed areas of the globe, or in Communist areas, is hampered to an even greater extent by a scarcity of reliable, comparable data. Until recently, for instance, Brazil's "consumer price index"—published regularly in such places as the IMF's "International Financial Statistics"—was actually an index only for consumer prices in the city of Rio de Janeiro. To make matters worse, the index did not include housing prices. These had been removed from the index in the late 1960s, at a time when Brazilian officials were under much criticism for failing to bring down the country's high rate of inflation. Housing prices, as it happened, were among the most swiftly rising prices in the index. Their removal, done without publicity, naturally slowed the rise of the index and made Brazil's entire inflation picture appear a good deal brighter than it really was.

Brazilian officials have taken steps recently to improve the accuracy of their economic statistics, including their price gauges. Apparently, the country has made some real progress in its battle to reduce inflation. However, many other less-developed countries, without Brazil's resources, still issue crude, unreliable data that should be treated with much skepticism but is carried in IMF publications and elsewhere.

Such data should nonetheless not be disregarded out of hand. The economic importance of such countries is bound to increase further in coming years. As economic information about the world around us continues to improve, our understanding of the U.S. economy, as well as of other economies, should inevitably grow. As Brazil has recently attempted to improve its statistics, so other countries will surely also begin to provide more and better economic information about themselves. This, of course, is all to the good. For on the economic front, as on other fronts, we can no longer afford simply to survey the U.S. scene by itself. A broader view is required.

# INDEX

**201**

Gross national product, real, 31,
44, 47-49, 67, 73, 87, 116-117,
170-171, 192
as economic gauge, 22-24
as growth measure, 70
and money supply, 137
and potential GNP, 52-55
Grove, David, 165
*Gulag Archipelago,* 85

Harris Trust Co., 168
Harvard University, 65, 87
ABC curves of, 127-128
Harwood, Edward C., 179-181
Heebner, A. Gilbert
on forecasting, 168-169
on policy makers, 79
"Hot money," 58
Humphrey, Hubert, 175-176
Hupp Corp., 77

Indicators, coincident, 129-130,
158-159
Indicators, lagging, 129-130, 158-
159
Indicators, leading
distortion of, 170
international, 194
types of, 120-163
Industrial materials index, 33, 156
Industrial pollution, 43-44
Industrial production, 70-71, 87
Inflation, 25, 145
in Germany, 158
tendency towards, 105-111
transmission of, 186-187
Interest rates, 144-146
and stock prices, 151
as lagging indicator, 159
International Business Machines,
165

*International Financial Statistics,* 196
International Monetary Fund,
193, 196, 198-199
Inventories, 82
and economic cycles, 73-77
as leading indicator, 156
Ireland, 194
Italy, 191, 198

Japan, 46
economic indicators of, 194-195
productivity in, 49-50, 56-60
real GNP in, 192
slump in, 191
Job vacancies, 15
Johnson, Lyndon B., 65, 81, 175

Kennecott Copper Corp., 30
Keynes, John Maynard, 147
Klein, Lawrence, 168
Klein, Philip A., 194
Kondratyev, Nicolai D., and Kon-
dratyev Wave, 83-87
Kuznets, Simon, 87

Labor costs
and productivity, 49
in recessions, 110
and wages, 86
Labor Department, 9
Layoff rate, 156, 162
Living standards, 73
and productivity, 48-49
measurement of, 35-42
"social" factors in, 42-44
Loan demand, 151
*Los Angeles Times, The,* 166

Manufacturers Hanover Trust, 3,
79, 165
Massachusetts Institute of Technology, 20

# 206

Project Link, 195
Prudential Life Insurance Co., 165

Quit rate, 127

RCA Corp., 165
Recessions, 87, 110, 161, 172, 191
  history of, 63-68
  old saw about, 9
  and unemployment, 18
Reeder, Charles, 168
Regan, Donald T., 172-173
Reich, Charles, 108
Reserve requirements, 134-135
Roosevelt, Franklin D., 91, 129
Russia, 193

St. Lawrence University, 177
Samuelson, Paul A.
  on gross national product, 20
  on the stock market, 150-152
Schmiedeskamp, Jay, 125
Schroder Naess & Thomas, 74
Schultz, Harry D., 177-179
Schwartz, Anna, 140
*Scientific American,* 128, 163
Sears, Roebuck and Co., 48
Selden, Richard T., 107-108
Services, 21, 69, 100-105
Shilling, A. Gary, 168, 170, 171-173, 180
Shiskin, Julius, 155
  on stock prices, 150-151
  on unemployment, 13-14
Solzhenitsyn, Aleksandr I., 85
Sommers, Albert T., 115, 117
Spencer Trask & Co., 29, 153
Sprinkel, Beryl W., 168
"Stagflation," 137
Stalin, Josef, 85-86
Standard & Poor's Stock Index, 149-150, 152

Stanford University, 109
Stein, Herbert, 87-88, 174
Stock prices, 139-140, 178
  as leading indicator, 128-129, 149-154
Swarthmore College, 177
Sweden, 49, 194

Taxation, 78, 95-96
Time deposits, 133
Towers, Perrin, Forster & Crosby, 28
Trade, balance of, 187-188, 195
  and gross national product, 21
  significance of, 58-60
Transfer payments, 90-100
Treasury Department, 3, 9, 143

Unemployment insurance, 98-99
Unemployment rate, 9-12, 53, 82, 160, 176, 181
  and "discomfort" index, 41
  makeup of, 13-15
  worsening of, 111-113
Unions, labor
  membership in, 104-105
  power of, 110
United Nations, 196
University of Chicago, 137
University of Michigan, 124
University of Pennsylvania, 177, 195
University of Virginia, 107
*U.S. News & World Report,* 14
U.S. Trust Co., 168

"Vendor performance," 148
Von Hayek, Friedrich A., 114-115
Von Hoffman, Nicholas, 6-7

Walker, Charls E., 3-4
*Wall Street Journal, The,* 2, 5, 13,